Sylvia provides readers with her experiences in caring for her aging mother. She vividly describes her emotions as she navigates the challenges, she faces in supporting her beloved mother. It is a journey many of us travel and it is helpful to know we are not alone. Sylvia is a gifted and compassionate author.

—*Geneva Escobedo author of Dichos de mi Padre/ Sayings of my Father and Reflections of the Heart. Stories and Poems from Life.*

Sylvia, author of *Unraveled-Journey Led by Faith and Hope*, uses her conversational style of writing to engage readers in her personal struggle of caring for an elderly parent. She shares her intimate experience of a situation many of us are familiar with. Sylvia's worries are heightened as she maneuvers the struggles of the unknown as she deals with an aging parent with declining health. As their roles become reversed, she grieves the loss of the concept of a strong mother she once loved and admired. In her usual vivid language sprinkled with humor, she allows us inside her world of doubt, fear, and uncertainties in this universal dilemma of caretaking.

—*Flora Gamez Grateron, Author of Through the Door, Cuentos de Casa and Open Doors, Cuentos de Familia.*

Just as she did in her first book, in her newest one, Sylvia opens her life and heart to her audience and fearlessly shares what she's endured and learned throughout her interesting life as a Mexican American woman living in the Borderlands. In her newest exploration of her experiences, Sylvia broaches the common experience of elder care. She reveals the vulnerabilities, fears, and triumphs of a deeply loving mother-daughter relationship. Sylvia writes about pain, suffering, loss, and love with a gentle but experienced hand that assures the reader they are not alone in whatever journey they may be on. This is another lovely work.

—*Andrea Hernandez Holm, Author of Not Enough, Too Much*

"I enjoyed this quite a bit, as Sylvia helped her mother evolve into a real person as she approached old age. Sylvia's approach surely helped her readers adjust to the caregiver role as a parent ages."
—*Bill Worth is a retired newspaper editor who now writes fiction and does copy-editing. His novels are House of the Sun: A Metaphysical Novel of Maui, and The Hidden Life of Jesus Christ: A Memoir, www.billworthbooks.com.*

Note: All endorsers' books can be found on Amazon.com (soft-cover, kindle).

Yearning for Mamá

The One From Yesteryear

Sylvia R. Merino

ISBN: 979-8-89079-190-0 (paperback)
ISBN: 979-8-89079-189-4 (ebook)

Table of Contents

Introduction vii

Surrendering to Obedience 1

A Man's Tenderness And Patience 6

Free Yet Lonely 9

The Silent Illness 14

Life Pleasures Diminish 19

COVID Keeps Us Away 23

The Cocktail Cure 33

Immigration Takes Her Away 36

The Bed Couch 41

Pet Peeves 43

The Warning Causes a Domino Effect 50

Mother of All Saints 57

Unstable But Trying 66

Knot on Forehead, Subtle Mistakes 70

The Finger 75

Solving the Puzzle, Not With the Gummy. 79

The Mysterious Fall. 82

Is It Only Mamá? 85

Mamá's Hair 93

Reflections 97

Gatherings 102

Memory and Sneaky 107

The Daughter Visits 117

Smart Electronics – Not For Some. 120

Fear of Tomorrow 125

Introduction

At the beginning, there was guilt and shame as I selfishly thought of the loss of my everyday pleasures. *"Am I even the right one to care for mamá?"* These were my first thoughts. I was worried even before I experienced one day of care. *"I, the one who worries about everything and anything, and now I have mamá to worry about."* I worry about not being a good caregiver. I worry that I won't know what to do when she tells me she's not feeling well. I will worry on the days she's in pain and I can't do anything about it. I worry that I'm not patient. And I will worry when I'm with Mom, about everything waiting for me at my own home: chores, bills, keeping the house clean, and all the materialistic things.

Just recently, I realized that my fears are that of denial. Denial that Mom could be leaving us soon. Denial that Mom can't do things for herself that she used to do with strength and stamina. Denial that Mom has her own fears. Denial that Mom is no longer the mother of yesterday.

Our parents age and eventually become ill and dependent. We either send them to a nursing home, or we care for them. In the Mexican culture most families have a designated child (usually the youngest daughter) who will care for elderly parents. I'm sure that has changed throughout the years but in my family, a nursing home couldn't even be a thought.

After Mom's many falls, additional care was required. I have struggled throughout her care. I give much credit to those whose profession is caregiving. I don't know how they go about doing this day after day. It is also trying when something non-medical arises, things that are not part of a licensed caregiver, but they are for my siblings and me. I wasn't trained and must continue learning as I go. I become emotional, sad, and sometimes angry. Angry because I have thoughts that I am failing her. *"Did she fail me?"* Surely not, because here I am writing my second story. It is because of her and my dad that I can do this. Even through all my insecurities, I owe it to her. Mom also carried insecurities when I was born and through my teens. I was different from my older sister. What she learned from my sister's first years would not be the same with me, but she raised me the best she knew how and went on to raise four more with their unique personalities. She wasn't a perfect mother and I'm not a perfect daughter. With that in mind, I will continue to learn the profession of caregiving, without the schooling, but with the guidance of my family and friends who have gone through this with their own parents. Mom, I am sure, is also feeling frustrated and sad as she slowly loses her independence and requires more assistance.

My story is that of my feelings, my frustrations, and trials I am put through. The story is of Mom and her antics. The story is of Mom's friends, the doctors and even the paramedics. The story is of her children wanting the best for her whether they are hands-on, or from afar. The story is of caring for a mom who can be difficult at times, yet we love her just the same.

Finally, the story is of me, the caregiver, and losing my role as a daughter. Throughout her care, I mourn for the mom of long ago, the mother who gave birth to me and raised me. I prefer the mom who reprimanded me for misbehaving, and the one who pointed out my flaws even though that hurt. I struggle, as the mom from long ago becomes more and more the patient, and I the caregiver — and no longer the daughter.

Surrendering to Obedience

"Oh, how assuming to think I am the right one.
To take my mamá's hands instead of her taking mine.
Who am I to be entrusted to care for mamá, singled
out from amongst her six children.
"Why? Who am I?"
– Sylvia R. Merino

"*I guess it will be Sylvia. Her job is flexible.*" The words are unsaid, but I hear them. They resonate with my total being. It is September of 2001 when my husband, Ralph; our daughter, Melissa, and I move back to Tucson from Berthoud, Colorado. I work from home, but Mom assumes I'm not working, even though I am working more hours than I ever have. And worse, I sense that I will be laid off very soon.

"Why me? I didn't ask for this." I say this to myself, as I am designated Mom's caregiver. Initially, I felt like I was having

tantrums. *"How can I care for her when I am feeling physical pain and fatigue?"* I'm already feeling resentful without knowing what it will really take to care for Mom. I don't like feeling sorry for myself, so I think at this point I'm just being stubborn.

Fortunately, years later when her condition worsened, my Rheumatoid Arthritis pains diminished, by the grace of God who led me to a naturopathic doctor. Thinking back, it was the worry of trying to care for Mom before caring for myself. I have often heard that one must care for oneself first to be able to care for others. I did struggle with pain earlier, and so it was very hard caring for mom at the same time. But somehow, I survived it.

It used to be that even when Mom was well, I couldn't be in her home for more than 15 minutes at a time. It may have been something about my younger years or the fact that she didn't like to be interrupted from her TV time. Mom is a good lady; many mention her kindness. Some even call her Santa Teresita (St. Therese). Mom's name is Teresa. I agree that she is kind. She is not a jealous person nor is she greedy. But she is stern, stubborn, feisty, ornery, and sometimes too honest. When I was a child, we didn't get angry with each other, nor did we have screaming matches. I don't know of a perfect mother. I'm not a perfect mother and I'm sure my daughter would have a story to tell!

As an adult, I once came out and told Mom about some of her hurtful comments. She apologized profusely and said she didn't have the resources as we do today. Sometimes she'll randomly sigh and tell me how wrong she was. My hurts are petty things such as her pointing out my black knees or my awful thick hair that in her eyes could never look nice. Today it is more of an annoyance as she points out my flaws. For example, she is constantly asking me about that big rash above my elbow. It's been there for years. As a child, I used to pick my skin when I was nervous just like the kids who bite their nails. She still questions my black knees. My legs are very light, but my knees are dark. In the summer, I tried applying sunblock on them so that the dark knees could blend in with my tanned legs, but the sunblock wore off before

I could step outside, so that didn't work for me. I'm in my late 60's now, so I really don't care if my knees are black or blue. Most of the time, I just ignore the comments or make a joke out of them, and we all laugh. I always felt ugly and worthless, but I don't feel that way anymore. I was too sensitive then and still am today, but today I understand that her negative comments are not intentional. *"So why am I worried?"*

Mom's mind was sharp at the beginning of my new caregiving role. We were able to communicate while we sat in the doctor's waiting room because Mom still had ideas and goals, especially with her sewing and knitting. She always had someone in mind for that new blanket she was knitting. I would drive her to Walmart or Hancock's so she could pick out the pattern and fabric for the toddler's dress she had in mind. Today, taking her to her doctor's visits is different. We sit in the car mostly in silence as I drive. At the doctor's office both of our minds are focused on Mom's condition and the doctor's analysis and answering the doctor's questions. On the way home, I glance at Mom as she sits with her hands folded on her lap. She stares ahead silently. I'll ask her what she's thinking about, and she'll give me an answer, or I'll see her lips quiver, but nothing comes out. My stomach feels pressure because I swallow sadness, and the feelings of frustration that there is nothing I can do for her. As always, I try to talk about something funny to at least make her laugh. Most of the time I succeed, but that is only a Band-Aid or distraction to cover up what she is not telling me.

One time when it became unbearable caring for Mom after one of her falls, my siblings and I had thoughts of putting Mom in an assisted-living home, until a friend and I went to visit a mutual friend at a nursing home. The woman had broken her hip and had very little physical therapy. She never gained strength to fully walk again, so she was bound to a wheelchair. When we walked through the doors of this home, there were nurses sitting in the living room eating their lunch, talking and laughing. One directed us to her room where we found her sitting up in bed. She appeared to be happy, but you could see she was lonely. She used to read novels, but I don't recall seeing books in her room. She had some family pictures on a small shelf that she quickly pointed out for us to look at. Her eyes lit up when she talked about her family who had visited recently. She had a TV that was turned off. She didn't know we were coming to visit, so I wondered if it was normal to lie in bed staring into space.

It saddened me to see an older woman next door, possibly in her late nineties. She was sitting in a chair positioned at the opening of her bedroom door. Her head was down as if she were looking for something on the floor. She looked very sad. She didn't acknowledge our presence; she was in her own zone. Perhaps she was thinking of her past life, or she was dreaming of the family she had outside this home; one who rarely visited.

We didn't stay for long. We said our good-byes and left the home with a bad taste in our mouths. We wondered why the nurses weren't making time to be with these ladies. Maybe they did when not having their lunch. I didn't want to judge, but what we saw was sad. I knew then that I would never leave Mom in a place where she would be neglected or harmed.

The difference between a caregiver caring for a stranger versus someone they've lived with is that they don't know the patient's background, their history, or even their personality. I can't even fathom how that caregiver can begin to guess how the patient would respond or react to a simple action of a touch on the shoulder if that person was not used to receiving or giving affection. And how about eating patterns? Do these caregivers feed these strangers what they think is good for them as taught in school, or do they go by what the patient prefers? All these thoughts make me crazy. So, yes, I would rather care for Mom, the person I know.

I am sure there are very good nursing homes with good nurses and staff. In each of the negative stories I hear, it involves younger employees. If they went to school to become a licensed caregiver, were they not taught to have good bed-side manners? Were they not taught how to respect people of all genders, sizes, and color, and especially the vulnerable?

So now it was up to me to learn patience, learn to deal with pettiness and get on to the task of caring for Mom. I am no longer her daughter, and she is no longer Mom. I am the caregiver; she is the patient. I surrender to obeying the call of being her caregiver, not because I was chosen, but because with love all can be done.

A Man's Tenderness And Patience

"He comes and he goes, caring for his father.
Gentle hands, loving heart.
Patience, patience.
His sister is the nurse, his brother,
the gardener, His wife, *la* señora."
– Sylvia R. Merino

Patience is not my virtue. It never has been, so I am a lot like Mom. Mom wants things done right now. Sometimes it means that I drop the bags in my arms on the closest couch or counter to tend to her needs. When I ask my husband Ralph for a favor like to bring me a glass of water because he is in the kitchen, he gladly does it, but sometimes I wait for more minutes than I wish to wait, and so I get up to get my own water. "Be patient," he tells me. He is the master of patience. He was also his dad's caregiver, and a very patient one.

Ralph had recently retired and was looking forward to his hobbies and maintaining our home, things he had put on the back burner until he retired. Unfortunately, my father-in-law developed knee pain due to bone rubbing against bone. He refused to have surgery, and so as time went by, he eventually became wheelchair-bound. Even with his painful knees, for the longest time, he continued to work in his yard. He would dig trenches for hours. He would make or build "tata inventions" as Ralph's family calls them. These are inventions for something needed, but not having the required material he improvised with what he had. He worked so hard all his life, so he wasn't going to let the pain stop him from doing what he loved to do. He was a cowboy in his early years, then worked at the San Manual, Magma Copper Mine in San Manual, AZ until he retired. He loved to dance. Bea, my sister-in-law, would have him out on the dance floor at weddings, birthday parties and even in their kitchen after a Christmas or New Year's dinner, and later would move him around in dance moves as he sat in his wheelchair.

When his driver's license was due for renewal, he was taken to the local Department of Motor Vehicle (DMV). While the DMV administrator was preparing the paperwork, my father-in-law mentioned that he didn't need a license. He knew that he could be a danger to himself and others. My sister-in-law explained to him that it was an ID he was getting, not a license.

He was losing his balance, and the knee pain was excruciating. Then came the time when he could no longer walk on his own. He was bedridden and was in a wheelchair for his meals and when taken outside to enjoy the warm weather.

Ralph and his siblings began to experience caregiving. His sister is a retired ER (Emergency Room) nurse. With more than 40 years of experience, she knows the medical side of caregiving. Ralph and his siblings did what they could to help physically and of course it came with emotions for all of them, including my mother-in-law.

At night Ralph set his alarm clock to awaken him every hour so he could check on his dad. After his dad passed away, it took him months to get back to his normal sleep schedule. They didn't repeat this with my mother-in-law because she sadly passed away soon after from COVID. What I learned and observed is that Ralph was kind, loving, tender, and a very patient man with the care he gave his dad for almost two years.

I will learn to be patient and loving. Ralph is my example, and my prayers will keep me out of trouble.

Free Yet Lonely

"Mamá, the strong woman.
She keeps her composure as her love lies in
eternal sleep. She calls the closest daughter
to come help. The daughter calls for
help. She knows something is very wrong.
Papá is gone."
– Sylvia R. Merino

Before Mom went into depression in early 2012, she was living by herself. Dad had passed away in June of 2004 and from then on Mom had no problem staying alone and sleeping alone. She walked to church every morning. She cooked, washed, and cleaned. She went out to eat with friends, and she had people coming in and out of the house since she continued to sew for original clients from Lincoln Street, here in Tucson, Arizona where she lived most of her life. She continued to alter their clothes or sew simple dresses or pants. She used to sew bridesmaids' dresses, and even bridal gowns. As the years went by, she preferred to sew young or toddler girl's dresses or alter women's dresses and men's

9

shirts and slacks. The big gowns were too much for her during and after her depression.

**One of the last pictures of Mom and Dad together,
Father's Day, June 2004.**

The morning when dad passed away, Mom had walked to church to attend the 8 a.m. mass. The routine was to go to church and walk back home to make dad's breakfast. She always found him sitting on the couch meditating. I don't recall him watching TV that early so he would just sit very quietly, waiting on Mom. This morning Dad was not waiting, so Mom checked his room, and he was not in bed. The bathroom door was opened and to her surprise and horror she found Dad lying between the toilet and shower. Mom called Laura. "Se cayó tu papá y no puedo levantarlo." ("Your dad fell, and I can't pick him up.") Laura went as quickly as she could to help Mom pick up dad. When she arrived, she was devastated when she saw that Dad was dead. She immediately called the paramedics. To this day, when my aunt calls her to help pick up Mom after a fall, she asks, "Is she dead?" Of course, it is now something to laugh about, but nothing close to what Laura felt that day when she arrived at Mom's.

After Dad's funeral services and everything calmed down, we thought Mom would get lonely and depressed, but she fooled us. She refused to move in with any of her adult children. She continued with her routine, but she now had friends picking her up for lunch or for church activities. She even went on a trip abroad to the Holy Land. In a nutshell, she was energetic and participated in all activities with the other members. Other than me, she didn't know anyone but the priest, who was the director of this trip. I injured one of my knees during the first event, so I sat in the bus with an ice bag on my knee for most of the trip. Mom did fantastic on her own with a group of people she barely knew.

Mom and me at (and in) the Dead Sea.
This is when we were in Israel. It was cold!

Mom felt freedom for the first time. She was no longer tied to a routine like having Dad's meals on the table by a specific time. She didn't need to ask for anyone's permission to go to church meetings or to go out to lunch with a friend. Sometimes her absence was a worry. She didn't have a cell phone at that time, so if she didn't answer the house phone, we immediately thought she fell and couldn't get up or that something worse had happened. When this occurred, my sister or I would drive to her house to check on her only to find an empty house. Eventually, she learned to alert us when she was leaving with friends.

Mom continued to cook for herself. I caught on that when she didn't see us for a couple of days, she would cook *caldo* (vegetable with beef soup) or chile relleno, or something she knew we would happily pick up after work. It didn't occur to us that she was feeling lonely, and that food was her bait to get us to her house for a visit. After a while it was becoming too frequent, but we didn't want to hurt her feelings so some evenings when I worked super late hours, I wouldn't show up until after dark. I tried to delicately tell her that some days I work very late hours and can't always make it to her home before dark. She continued to call us to pick up dinner and to pick up groceries or a prescription. This pattern changed when she became more tuned to the new TV programs. My siblings and I began visiting her more often on weekends. After retirement we began visiting more often during the week.

This is an old picture of my parents' children and grandchildren. This picture is prior to the great grandchildren. (Spring 2004)

The Silent Illness

"Mamá is gone, not physically.
She can't sleep or eat.
Everything frightens her, she's anxious.
She doesn't know why and neither do I."
– Sylvia R. Merino

Initially, Mom had many friends who kept her occupied. Then one of her best friends who drove her around passed away. Then another friend ended up needing to care for her husband so that meant less time visiting with Mom. Slowly Mom was losing contact with those she interacted with. I'm not sure if this is what triggered her depression, but now that I look back it is about the same time that she was losing her friends.

Shortly after returning from the Holy Land, Mom began to get anxious about everything, lost sleep, and was eating less. She stopped walking to church. She also required many trips to the hospital because everything she saw on TV that was an illness, she thought she had. She was becoming a hypochondriac.

The depression got worse, but at this point we had no idea it was depression she was going through. We were all learning as the days got harder. I'm still working and worry as I take time off to take Mom to the hospital or to appointments. Eventually, the emergency hospital staff recognized her and told her there wasn't anything they could do for her. When I refused to take Mom for a symptom that was the same as a time before, she would call Cecilia, a friend, to ask her to take her to the hospital. I had to explain that the hospital won't do anything for her. It was heartbreaking when Mom felt like she needed to go behind our backs. It's not that she was being sneaky, but she just couldn't understand why we refused to take her to the hospital. The emergency doctors couldn't find anything physically wrong with her.

Seeing her decline, day after day, was heart breaking. I didn't know what to do for her. The doctors didn't know what to do. We also took her to a naturopathic doctor's practice, and they were also frustrated when they couldn't find anything and stopped responding to our calls.

She didn't want anyone at her home. She was anxious. Everything was too much for her. One day, she told me that she wished something bad would happen to her physically so that she would end up at a hospital where she could finally sleep all day and all night.

Thank God for Cecilia, the friend who helps us with Mom. She is so special. She not only helps with Mom, but she has told us stories of others who call on her at all times of the day or night. She doesn't hesitate to help. She loves Mom and never refuses to help us. If she has an appointment or social plans, she feels badly that she must refuse, and she should not. We fully understand that she also has a life of her own.

During Mom's depression, we learned she was thinking her life was coming to an end. Not that she was telling us that, but it was through her actions and comments. For example, she started giving her good pots and dishes away. She had an old antique grinder that she brought with her from Rayón, Mexico, her hometown. My sisters and I wanted that grinder, but she doesn't remember giving it away. I looked all over my home, thinking she had given it to me, and maybe I forgot where I put it. She also gave away a nice stone baking pan and later she went crazy looking for it. Who knows who she gave it to? I bought her a new one. She also didn't want to buy things she needed in her home. She would ask, "Why? I won't be here for long."

As Mom started receiving invoices for all her doctors' and hospital visits, it wasn't easing her anxieties, it was making it worse. Fortunately, one of my sisters-in-law suggested we take her to a neurologist where her sister worked. With a referral from her PA, off we went to the neurologist a few days later. When the neurologist saw her, he immediately saw depression written all over her. I won't ever forget this moment. Mom was sitting on the table (bed) facing the doctor, and Stephen, my youngest brother, was sitting in one corner, and I was on the opposite side of the room. The neurologist looked into her eyes and asked her if someone was hurting her at home and she quietly said, "No.". Then he asked her if she was sad about something, and she burst into tears. She was sobbing and at the same time the doctor is telling her she needed to see a psychiatrist. He recommended a Spanish-speaking psychiatrist and prescribed her a small dose of an anxiety pill in a small quantity until she could see the psychiatrist. The first night she took the pill she slept through the night. During the day, she was still anxious and not eating as well. She wasn't the same Mom. She was quiet and stared at the TV screen not really watching what was on.

We were fortunate to get in to see the psychiatrist within a week or so. I was allowed to sit in during Mom's meeting. The psychiatrist explained to Mom that she wasn't the cause of the depression. It was something a large percentage of elderly people get. She explained the medical reasons. It has to do with decreased brain volumes in the frontal and temporal areas. She stressed that with Mom it was frontal and kept pointing at her forehead directly centered above her nose. This was all after she tested her memory and questioned her about her life. Did something happen to you in the past? Did someone hurt you, etc.? She prescribed a depression medicine and a different anxiety pill. The depression pill was to take effect after so many weeks of her taking it as prescribed. Sure enough, she eventually began turning back to her old self.

The psychiatrist also stressed she maintain a social life and became more active through going for walks and other activities she enjoys. Mom knits and continued knitting during her depression. We bought her yarn and told her someone was having a baby and needed a baby sweater and blanket. This was true since this is when all her grandchildren were beginning to have their own babies. Laura, my younger sister, had her make aprons for the older grandchildren or Halloween costumes, anything to keep her mind busy. By the time I had her sew some placemats for Christmas gifts, she was overwhelmed with all the requests and my placemats were ruined. I never told her that they came out crooked or unmatched. It doesn't matter because I can reuse the fabric for quilting.

The Mother's Day after her healing I wrote her the following letter. *(Also included in my first book: Unraveled – A Journey Led by Faith and Hope).*

"Dear Mamá,

This Mother's Day is different. After your suffering last year, I am grateful for your good health. It made me sad to see you downhearted. You, the mother who never tires.

For months we saw you hiding in a cave or bubble. I'd get angry sometimes. Anxiety came from not knowing how to cure you. My smile when with you, hid my sadness. I didn't want to cause you more pain.

This Mother's Day is different. Today we celebrate the days that brought you back, to the mamá we know.

God took care of you when I couldn't take any more. When our work came first, your friends stepped in. Thank you for not faulting me on those days when I couldn't help you.

You think I don't pray, but my prayers kept me sane when it hurt to look at you, the stranger, in depression. My heart died and I moved like a robot as I took you to the emergency room, or took you to this doctor, or that specialist, knowing you would be turned away with no diagnosis.

Thanks to Dr. Pelayo who spoke to you with tenderness while you sat hunched over without looking at her. She told us depression can come as a part of aging.

What happiness when you started taking the medications prescribed to you. You blossomed into the mother we knew, opening like the petals of a flower blooming one by one, day by day. You finally ate, slept, walked. When yelling and scolding came, we knew you were well, maybe not 100% well, but our mother was back!!

Thank God for doctors, your friends and for the patience He gave us, but we are most grateful for having you back as our mamá, the mother we know and love. Love, Sylvia."

Life Pleasures Diminish

"Mamá is too excited, she
runs out with her friends and
stumbles. She is hurting, hurting.
Doesn't know where."
– Sylvia R. Merino

Mom continued to see the psychiatrist until she felt she no longer needed her. Mom was back to herself, living as she did before the depression. She was so full of life and that made all of us happy and relieved, until she broke her femur. She had gone to our old parish, St. John the Evangelist, for a friend's funeral. On the way out, one of her friends mentioned that they had arrived in an antique car. All the women went running out to see the car and Mom stumbled on one of the parking lot cement blocks. I received a call from one of my family members that Mom was transported to the hospital and that I should go be with her. Cecilia had been with her, and so I took over so that Cecilia could go home. The nurses explained her injuries, and to our surprise the doctor who would perform her surgery was the same doctor who took care of fixing the meniscus tears of both my knees. I knew Mom would be in good hands.

After the surgery, Mom was transported to a rehabilitation facility for two weeks. I would never take her to this place again. For the most part, the staff were kind, but two incidents occurred. Mom may not speak good English, but she understands it well. By now, she also knew what medicines she needed to take. I visited her every day after work. One evening I walked in, and she said, "The night nurse isn't giving me all my medicines. They think I don't know what I take, and they don't believe me. And don't complain, just tell them which medicines I need to take at night."

On my way out, I went to the nurse's station and mentioned to her about the medicine incident. She had me fill out a complaint form per their protocol. The nurse was nice about it and apologized.

The next day when I arrived, I slowly walked into her room. I suddenly stopped when I heard the young nurse shouting at my mom. "*Siéntate*!" "Sit down!" Mom was trying to go to the restroom and the nurse was helping her sit down. Mom was slow because of the surgery but the nurse was yelling at her with persistence. I quickly walked over and surprised her.

"Mom isn't deaf, she can hear you. I'll take over," I said, and she left.

"Don't complain!" Mom yells at me as I walk towards the door to leave. Same routine, but this time I went to the staff desk and was asked to fill out the complaint form. The next evening when I visit Mom, she said, "I know you complained because everyone has been treating me so nice!" I laughed and explained that it is critical to complain or point out issues so that the senior nurses and staff can better train the new nurses. She was fine for the rest of the time, but I was always on edge and worried about how she was being treated when family wasn't present. For the two weeks, my siblings, and aunt visited her and so did our parish priest. If I missed one night, I felt guilty the whole next day.

When she was discharged, I took her home and we asked Chalita, Mom's cousin, if she would stay with her until she was stable on her feet. She had a nurse come by to ensure her house was safe. Then an occupational therapist, and a physical therapist came regularly. The occupational therapist encouraged her to do everything she needed on her own with limited help. We were surprised that Mom was recovering quickly. Chalita stayed with her on Tuesdays through Thursday night. I set up schedules for Mondays, Fridays, Saturdays and Sundays with our siblings, an aunt, and Cecilia. When Chalita left her shift, Mom managed on her own throughout the day. We took her food so that she wouldn't need to cook for herself. The occupational therapist wanted her in the kitchen, so we let Mom fix her own breakfast and she did just fine. This setup ran smoothly for about a year. Then Chalita and Mom were bumping heads. Chalita was trying to follow the therapists' instructions with Mom, but Mom had her own stubborn ideas and refused to listen to Chalita or anyone of us.

At this time of Mom's life, she can think for herself and knows that what we are reminding her to do, like the exercises and the taking of pills regularly, are orders from medical professionals. I can deal with Mom, especially when she gets ornery or stubborn. Sometimes I just need to remind her that the doctor will ask why she didn't follow the post-op instructions. Mom then sheepishly obeys.

Mom started giving Chalita the cold shoulder until one night when Mom fell out of bed. Mom is dead weight, and so she stays where she falls until someone strong picks her up. Since it was late at night, Chalita had to pick her up alone. She wrapped a sheet slightly above her stomach to pull her up. This tired Chalita, and Mom knew it. The next few days Mom was in a better mood and treated Chalita with more respect.

For whatever reason, I stayed at Mom's one night while Chalita was there. Mom had another fall and with the sheet and the two of us, we were able to get her back in bed. During these last falls, she was able to push herself up a little with her good leg.

Mom started complaining again about Chalita nagging her about what she should be doing regarding the therapists' instructions. Mom is also very picky about her food and makes everyone crazy trying to determine what to fix her for lunch and dinner. I had not yet experienced this part until a few years later. Chalita continued watching over her and finally Mom told her that she was back to normal and would stay home alone day and night. We did see improvements and she was doing more for herself. She was also taking her own showers without help. She pretty much healed.

COVID Keeps Us Away

"Mamá's stomach aches are a
repeat. The doctor says she's fine.
Makes the green chile salsa. She hurries,
slips, and falls. The ambulance
takes her away, far away. She's alone.
COVID keeps us away."
– Sylvia R. Merino

Mom was doing just fine. Her depression was under control. Her femur operation and recovery were behind her. She was feeling great. She was eating everything she loves to eat.

Then one day, in early June of 2020, Mom developed what she said was terrible stomach aches and she just knew it was a tumor or cancer. Her primary doctor had left the clinic, so she was now seeing a new Physician Assistant (PA) who knew little of Mom's history. The PA became concerned and scheduled a colonoscopy and an upper GI at the same time, and separately, a liver ultrasound.

She had previously been diagnosed with a hiatal hernia, so the gastroenterologist checked it to make sure it had not worsened, and during this procedure he diagnosed her with an overly acidic stomach that was exacerbating the hiatal hernia. She was told she could eat whatever she wants but to avoid acidic, spicy food. He prescribed her an antacid medication that she needed to take in the morning and before lunch for six weeks. After the six weeks she was put on omeprazole, one per day. This is exactly what she was told by a doctor six years prior. I had also diagnosed her symptoms when she first complained about her stomach pains. I would never want my evaluations to override the doctor's evaluation, but we could not encourage Mom to continue taking the omeprazole again. We also begged her to stop eating so much green chile. She was always eating small burritos with the roasted green chile peppers and strips of cheese wrapped in a tortilla. Even now, when she complains of a stomach pain, I ask her what she ate and it is always *nada,* nothing, until I tell her that she must have eaten chile or snuck a small soda. She can't have bubbly drinks either. I give her three Tums and within 30 minutes she feels better. My husband and I both have a hiatal hernia, so we understand the discomfort it causes.

The liver ultrasound was scheduled, and I sat with her while they were doing the test. It turns out she has a fatty liver but nothing serious enough for surgery or medication. She just needs to eat healthier. They, too, saw that she has a very acidic stomach as she was told by the gastroenterologist. She went home satisfied that she didn't have cancer. As usual, she's not happy that they can't make her well with a touch of a wand.

Things were calming down with Mom, when we get the call that Mom was in dad's room looking for something in one of the tall dressers. The bottom drawers were light so when she pulled on the full top drawer the dresser started falling towards her. Fortunately, the dresser landed on the bed and Mom fell on the carpet. She survived this fall. The dresser was replaced with a small nightstand.

A couple of weeks later, on June 25th, we invited Tía Amelia (Mom's sister) to dinner for her birthday. We also invited Laura, my sister, and her husband, Delbert. They were to pick Mom up since they live closer to her. Tía Amelia, my husband, and I are waiting for the rest to arrive. Instead, we receive a phone call from a very distressed Laura. "Mom fell, we just called 911." We sat in awe, and I saw my world go flying past me. I knew this meant something big, but at the time I didn't know how big.

This is how Mom fell. She had made her popular green chile salsa. Laura and Delbert picked her up. Laura thought she was doing the right thing by taking the salsa from Mom's hands and putting it in her car to then go back to help Mom out the door. She specifically told Mom, "I will be back to help you out the door." Mom, being hasty, ran to the door and slipped on the rug and fell on her side, all twisted. Delbert pulled her up and dragged her to the couch. The paramedics called for an ambulance and announced that because of COVID, no one would be allowed into the hospital. Laura and Delbert drove to our house, and we quietly ate our dinner. We discussed what we imagined the damages were and what it would take to care for her.

Mom had emergency surgery. Her left hip was replaced. She fractured her left shoulder and her left wrist. She was in the hospital for a couple of days and then was transported to a physical therapy facility of our choice. We chose a facility closer to our home that had good reviews. We were still not allowed to visit her. We worried because of her not speaking English. I received calls from the therapists and nurses, and they would each tell me what a joy Mom was to care for. I was thinking they had the wrong daughter, or they were talking about a different Mom! I'm joking, of course, as I know Mom would never treat anyone badly.

After a week, I was called to bring Mom clean clothes and pick up her dirty clothes. I was allowed to go to the emergency check-in desk but that is as far as they would let me in. This went on for three weeks. On the last day, I was allowed into her room.

I found her sitting in a wheelchair. She did look cute. The nurses crowded around us, and they went on to explain that she was a very good patient and that they understood each other perfectly well. I just rolled my eyes! She knows that I am being playful when I tease her with my smart remarks and actions.

The physical therapist came in and had me follow him to the exercise room. He showed her (and me) how to use a cane properly and which type of cane would be the best for her. She needed a multi-point cane. I called it a four-prong cane. For now, she was to use the single point cane the hospital gave her (surely the cost would be added to her bill).

One of the nurses took her in the wheelchair to the area where I would pick her up. Thank goodness because I would not have been able to push the wheelchair on my own. With that all done, I drove her home. All the way home, she commented about how great the nurses and staff were. Thank God that all went well, unlike the other place when she fractured her femur.

Chalita was called again for help. She grudgingly came, knowing she didn't have a choice. In the meantime, Mom was secretly calling Tía Fina (aka Josefina) who lives in Rayón, Sonora, Mexico. Tía Fina is Mom's younger sister. Her daughter, Lupita (aka Ana), my cousin, lives in Tucson with her husband and two boys. Tía Fina made occasional trips from Mexico to see Lupita and her grandchildren. She was talking about getting immigrated to the U.S. After so many of Mom's calls pleading for her to come live with her, Tía Fina decided to accept it. Lupita then worked to help her get immigrated. Shortly before all this, her husband (my uncle) passed away, so she was in mourning and ready to get away. Since it was during COVID, it took a few more months before the border was opened for travel. Chalita was more than happy to hear that Tía Fina would take over Mom's care. The news was also a happy occasion for me and, of course, for my siblings who were on the schedule to spend nights with her.

Tía Fina's travels kept getting delayed because of COVID and Chalita was now accepting a babysitting job with one of my nephew's daughters and later her newborns. She had an excuse to never stay with Mom again. This meant that I would take over Mom's care full-time, whether it meant from afar or staying overnight. Between Laura and me, we took Mom food to eat at lunch and/or dinner. Laura bought her groceries, I spent weeknights with her, and my brothers helped on Friday and Saturday. On the first night I stayed with her, I told her, "If you need something, don't yell with a demanding tone, instead, do it lovingly and don't forget to say please." Mom laughed and promised she would but that didn't last long. Mom had a habit of hollering at us when she needed something. She had a very demanding voice. I should have been used to it since it hadn't changed from our younger years. Now, as the years go by, and Mom is slowing down, so is her tone of voice. It saddens me to watch her slowly becoming meek.

One of the weekends before Tía Fina came and before we knew she would come for good, our family met at Mom's home. We also Face Timed with Richard, our brother, who lives in Minnesota. We discussed who would be the scheduler, and later the caregiver, for Mom. Everyone sat quietly. My stomach tightened as eyes landed on me. I was the one who was already handling her doctor visits and taking her to her appointments. I was still working full time, but to others, it didn't seem to matter because I was the one with the most flexible schedule. We tossed around ideas of hiring an outside agency or moving her to one of our homes, but we knew she would refuse.

It was decided that our sister Ana would take her dinner on Saturdays, enough for two meals. Laura would take her a breakfast burrito or lunch that she could also eat for dinner. We eventually hired a young girl who came a couple of days, but Mom decided she was too expensive and all she did was sit on the couch going through her cellphone. Cecilia would pop in when she could. Tía Amelia visited almost every day. There was another friend who would bring her food and visit with her, but she also needed to care for her ill husband and couldn't visit as often.

Chalita helped for a few days, until she needed to start caring for our great-nephews. Chalita was helping her with her shower and that was a big ordeal. Mom was too independent and hated people doing things for her. Eventually, though, she got used to the help.

Mom was sent home with a sling and a wrist band covering most of her hand. She kept the sling on for a while. It's amazing that with a sling and wrist band, she continued to knit. When the wrist band became too bothersome, she removed it. I bought her a smaller one that only went around her wrist, thus freeing her fingers. The sling slowly became too much for her and she decided to get rid of it, ignoring Chalita's pleas to leave it on.

Before the idea of Tía Fina coming to stay with Mom, we learned a few things about the two living together. I was taking notes, because I knew my day would come. Mom, as I mentioned before, is very demanding, or maybe the word is stubborn. She wants things done her way. She also does not like to eat leftovers the next day. She needs something new every day. She doesn't like soups and doesn't like vegetables. The only exception is her *caldo*, vegetable and beef soup. She will eat that soup and even freeze some to have later. She will also eat menudo (Mexican soup with hominy and cows' intestines). So, what does that leave for her to eat? Everything that is bad for her: sweets, tortillas, fried foods, and lots of protein but mainly beef. She always fasted on Wednesdays and Fridays. This means she has two small meals a day and no meat. As her health deteriorated, the doctors suggested she stop fasting but that was like talking to the wall. Now in her '90s, she doesn't do it as often.

Tía Fina finally arrives. Mom is ecstatic and my siblings and I are overjoyed. This means that the easy chores remain for us, such as buying groceries, since Mom nor my tía drive. As a break for Tía Fina from having to cook every meal, Laura and I continued to deliver a meal at least once a week. Ana continued to take them food until she found out that Mom was giving away her food after eating it for one meal, or frankly told her she didn't like it.

Sometimes throughout the time Tía Fina was caring for Mom before she immigrated, Lupita would alert us that our tía had an early laboratory appointment on her side of town so that required that Tía Fina would need to spend the night at Lupita's home. The way I understood, is that the lab results were then sent to her doctor in Mexico. She would be gone for just one night. Of course, the alert came to me since I am now the official caregiver and coordinator. I would stay the night with Mom. It was not a big deal, and in fact, this gave me a clue to how mom was doing during these longer overnight visits. Most of the time it was a relief to know that she was doing well considering all she had been through.

During the first two weeks of Tía Fina's arrival from Mexico, she had to get used to the routine — and so did Mom. The first shower with Tía Fina was the worst for Mom. Mom washes herself; she just needs help undressing and stepping into the shower. Once in, she can do the rest. She was embarrassed to be seen in the nude by her own family. She got used to Chalita. Now it was time to get used to her sister, Fina.

About two days after Tía Fina started caring for Mom, I went over to drop off some groceries. I looked at Mom and see her dress with food stains and noticed that she just looked messy. I was in a hurry because I was in the middle of working on edits of my first book and wanted to turn in the final manuscript soon. I needed a break so went to buy Mom's groceries and figured I would deliver them and leave. There was no reason to stay there. "Mom, when was the last day you showered?" I asked.

"She won't let me help her shower. She's been waiting for you," Tía Fina hollers from the kitchen.

Mom quickly gets up from her recliner and goes to the bathroom and tells me she's ready for help. "*Why didn't she call me two days ago that she needed me to help her with the shower,*" I thought. Mom is very assuming. She didn't think I was probably in a hurry. I explain that I'm not there to give her a shower and that Tía Fina could help her. Tía Fina explains that she's embarrassed for her to see her. "Mom, I can't believe you are embarrassed for your own sister to see you. She will only see your *nalgas (buttocks)*, and she has a butt too! What is the big deal?" Mom ignores me and steps into the shower and waits for me to remove her dress, pour shampoo on hair and soap up her washcloth. She had already turned the water on. I went ahead and helped her. Then I proceed with the routine of drying her and dressing her. She then sat on the couch so I can put lotion on her feet because she can't reach them. I continue combing her hair. I explain to Mom that I can't drive over every day to help her with her shower and that she needs to let her sister help. The shower business is settled, and all is good.

Before I get up to leave, I look down and see she has not taken her pills. I nag her about that, too, but she tells me they upset her stomach. I repeat with the same suggestion each time, "Sandwich the pills. Eat a spoonful of food or eat a small cookie if she had already eaten lunch, take the pills, and eat another spoonful of food or cookie." I try to back off, knowing that not taking them was not going to hurt her since she has skipped her medicines for a few days in a row in the past. That should not be a regular outcome, and it did take us a few very trying months to get her on a regular schedule.

Tía Fina has kept Mom's house immaculate. She cleans every day. She also loves the outdoors and keeps the garden nice with the flowers I buy them, or with the plants they receive for Mother's day, Christmas and other holidays. Tía Fina also walks every evening. She became friends with Cecilia so at least she has someone else for company, other than Mom.

Tía Fina is not only Mom's sister and caregiver but also her companion. When Tía Fina takes a break, she sits with Mom, and they chat about people from Rayón as they knit or crochet with the telenovela or the *Doctora* (like Judge Judy) on the TV in the background. About three times a day, with or without the Spanish EWTN Catholic station, they pray the rosary. Sometimes in the afternoon my Tía Amelia will go over to pray with them. If she can't, they pray over the phone with the speaker on. So, if you need prayers, they are the women to call on! Tía Fina is very quiet and very patient, but she too learned she needed to be forceful with Mom, especially when it comes to food and taking her medicines.

Tía Fina has a kidney disease and because of it, she eats very healthy and stays active. She needs an injection pertaining to the kidney disease every 15 days. Between Mom and Tía Amelia, they couldn't find anyone to inject her, so who do they designate? I inherited that new responsibility and the only experience I have is when the doctor who performed Mom's surgery had his nurse teach me how to inject Mom in the stomach with the medicine that would keep her from getting an infection. At least I had that two-minute lesson.

Initially, I relied on her to tell me when she needed the injection but then she would forget, and after a few missed days, I began putting her injection due dates on my calendar. This is easy, but I wonder what it's like for the professional caregivers, caring for multiple patients with different needs. The only difference is that for them, it is their sole job during their scheduled time. With me, I had a full-time job, so I had conference calls scheduled, and I had my personal doctor appointments and Mom's appointments and then there were the social commitments. And because I love my hobbies, I have writing group dates and later I began volunteering at the church painting pots and wine bottles to sell at two of our craft fairs, with the profit going to the school. There are times when I feel overwhelmed but then I think about Mom who must feel overwhelmed with all her new physical limitations.

Mom and tía Fina knitting, a daily ritual.

The Cocktail Cure

"Mamá time. I'm the caregiver.
Mamá won't take her omeprazole.
It's too much to remember. Doesn't want
to be bothered. Too many hospital
visits make her think twice."
– Sylvia R. Merino

After I retired from the medical company here in Tucson, I
had the time to become more familiar with Mom's medical
records and more proficient in Mom's medical care. I also keep
track of the vaccinations she's had and those she still needs. Her
medications were also organized, and I prayed that when I wasn't
around, Tía Fina would make sure she took them.

Things were going well until Mom started getting Urinary
Tract Infections (UTIs). This meant many trips to urgent care.
The nurses already know her and are very attentive. As soon as she
walks in, one of the nurses takes Mom from me and takes her into
the restroom to collect a urine sample. I watch her as she slowly
makes it to the restroom door. The nurse waits and eventually

knocks to ensure she's okay. In one year, she had about four or five UTIs. At one of the urgent care visits, the doctor suggested Mom take an antibacterial medicine for life. Since then, she has had maybe one or two infections in the last two years.

The infections are not what worried me. It was that Mom began getting the symptoms days before she told me. I have learned to read her facial expressions. I see pain written all over her face but then I think she's just having another anxiety episode, or she is stressing over her kids' life issues. I go home worried and in deep thought trying to figure her out. Then on the second or third day of the symptoms and when she can no longer take it, she calls me — always when it is most convenient for her. If I was at her house that morning, she wouldn't tell me about the UTI because she was watching her program. It would have been no problem to take her then. I would have preferred her announcing her infection at that time instead of after I got home and have put on my "a gusto" clothes. We use that term daily, meaning our comfortable evening clothes! Meaning bra off and throwing on a nightshirt, or in the winter the flannels. It's not really all about me. Mom hates waiting in a waiting room, so the disadvantage of the late urgent care visits is that it seems like suddenly everyone in town needs urgent care. During the day it is not as bad. But Mom enjoys her TV shows so much that she prefers to suffer than to call to get her checked! The worry is that the longer she holds the UTI pain, there could be bad consequences. The infection could travel to the kidneys, damaging them forever.

A couple of months later, Mom complains again about her stomach. It's on her right side. I study her and try to analyze what this pain is all about. She literally looked like she was dying, it hurt so much. I finally gave in and told her to get ready. "We are going to the hospital." She then gets this look like she's questioning the idea of going to the hospital. "I don't want to be responsible if you die on me for not taking you in." She doesn't react to my comment. She's so focused on that big disease or cancer that is growing in her stomach.

At the hospital, after blood work and a CT Scan, they find two things. She is not drinking enough water, and she has built up acid. They ask her if she's taking acid reflux medication, and she stares into space not answering. I explained that she doesn't take them regularly and that on top of that, she is not eating well. The doctor leaves and returns with a "cocktail" of a strong pink liquid in a cup, about a half of a measuring cup. It is a heavy dosage of an acid reflux medicine. They keep her in for another hour and by then she is well, no pain. They repeat once more that she must take her omeprazole daily and stop eating spicy food and cut back on caffeine. The caffeine was fine because she barely adds half a teaspoon into her cup, once in the morning. It's the spicy food that will ruin her.

Immigration Takes Her Away

"Mamá has company. Her sister is
here. Mamá can't contain her joy. Chalita
is joyful. She is now free. Mamá's children are
screaming with joy. Poor mamá, she thinks
they don't love her. But we do."
– Sylvia R. Merino

After Tía Fina received her immigration status, she was now free to come and go between countries. Since all her regular doctors are in Rayón and Hermosillo, she would have to leave Tucson for the appointments. I assumed she would travel to her appointment and return within the week, at the latest. Nope! That was not the case. The first time she left she was gone for almost two months. She decided to stay for the full Lenten season. Shortly after Easter she returned.

This is an example of how our world was turned upside down. Not only mine, but it affected my siblings, and Mom. Mom immediately says, "Oh, how I miss Fina." This is after the first day she is gone! My job is to make up a schedule as to who will stay with Mom at night. The night shifts are the hardest because there is always an event going on with one or the other. Both brothers, and my younger sister, enjoy watching their games and during the fall attending the U of A (University of Arizona) football games. The schedule was like what we followed after Chalita left and we were waiting for Tía Fina to arrive. I don't know why I feel guilty for inconveniencing my brothers, but I do, so I always had some kind of dessert for them to have at Mom's or to take home. I was spoiling them, yet they didn't get it as hard as Laura and I did. It's not that Mom is hard; it is that it is hard to leave behind whatever we were in the middle of doing in our personal lives. Then we have Tía Amelia who constantly forgets when her shifts are, even though the schedule has not changed.

Laura also takes her nightly turn and since our dad passed away, she has handled all of Mom's finances. She does her annual taxes and keeps her updated on her check balance and ensures her fire and property taxes are up to date. Since Laura has all her utilities and mortgage payments online, Mom only gets junk mail, apart from her banking and mortgage statements. The statements are so that she can see what her balances and detailed transactions are. When there is a large purchase or sometimes even a small purchase, she will ask if she has money. This is annoying to Laura especially when she must repeat, "Yes, you have money. You get paid twice a month and you don't buy anything outside of food and your utilities." The very next day if I'm going to Sam's Club to buy large packages of paper towels, toilet paper, or whatever, she will ask if she has money. I know of other elderly friends who have the same concern. Mom's worry is that she thinks that one day she'll be put into a nursing home, and she won't have the money to pay for her stay. Other times, she'll quickly offer the money for whatever is needed. She also prefers to have cash on hand to pay us for her groceries. When I buy something bigger than groceries, I talk her into writing a check instead of giving me cash.

Laura offered to do more to help me, so I gave her the task of organizing our mom's pills in a pill box and keeping track of when she needs refills. My job was to continue to ensure Mom was safe during the day. Laura continued taking her a breakfast burrito and she and I took turns with lunch. I made sure she had dinner. I also watered her indoor and outdoor plants. This meant driving to her house every day, at least three times, even on days that I would not stay the night.

Later, much later, I couldn't depend too much more on Laura. Tía Amelia fell taking out her garbage can and rolled down to the street pavement. She had a concussion, cut her head open and fractured a tiny bone on her spine. Since then, Laura has taken on the responsibility of caring for her.

When Laura leaves Tucson for a couple of days to take care of her grandchildren, I become anxious. She doesn't go as often now but when she does, I still feel that anxiety. This all means that either Mom makes her own breakfast, or I make an extra trip to help her with breakfast. I also make sure she has groceries since Laura usually buys her groceries on Mondays, the same day she refills her pill box. When Ralph and I leave for our vacations, Laura takes over. It doesn't bother her. She and I are quite different in how we go about caring for Mom. I'm the worrier and maybe if I wasn't so overly protective of Mom, I would be more at ease caring for her and everything that pertains to her well-being.

Every time Tía Fina leaves for more than a week, I need to overcome any thoughts of resentfulness. I put my life aside other than the few moments I get between caring for Mom. Laura and I tried numerous times to bring Mom to our homes for the day, but she refuses. When writing my first book, I was not totally focused on my writing. Part of me was the nagging feeling that I needed to get back to Mom whom I had left alone for a couple of hours.

While Mom is feeling well, I can leave her alone for two hours at a time, but three hours is pushing it. Sometimes she complains that I returned too soon. Painting pots is something I can squeeze in when there isn't anything else I need to accomplish at home between mother visits, but it is usually a rush job. It's amazing that during these short periods, my paintings are improving. Maybe it's God saying, "Take care of Mom, I'll take care of you."

While I suffer with RA, and because it is not physically noticeable, Mom doesn't know how difficult it is to handle two houses. On a normal day, I get to her house about two hours after her breakfast and the kitchen needs cleaning. There are dirty dishes and water or food spots on the floor from her wobbling to her chair carrying her food in one hand and the cane in the other. The floor around her recliner is regularly swept. When I help her with her shower it takes at least 45 minutes from going into the shower and back to her recliner all dressed. I then comb her hair and apply lotion to her legs and feet since she can't bend down. During her shower, I'll do the sweeping and vacuum the carpeted rooms. Then it's making sure the flowers in pots on her porch are watered, especially in the hot summer months. Then I go home and do my chores whether it's going through mail, washing, getting a grocery list together, figuring out what to cook so that I cook enough to take Mom two meals. Then I try to spend an hour or two on my crafts or writing, but I can't concentrate because it's all Mom in mind and heart. On the days when the routine is reversed, when I begin the day with my personal chores, I am already exhausted when I get to Mom's house. Those are the hardest times to be with Mom, and when I must pray for patience. Surprisingly, I do chill out as I walk into her home and do what I need to do, and I look forward to going to bed at a decent time because Mom likes to be asleep by 9 o'clock. I go to my dad's room, as we call it, and lie down. Sometimes I read or watch a Netflix movie from my phone. I find it relaxing, knowing it is "my" time plus it makes me feel like I am back home on Lincoln Street as a child.

I often think of the days when Mom was a clean fanatic. When she would go to Rayón for an extended stay, she would leave us to feed dad and make his lunch, sweep, and clean the bathrooms and kitchen. She would come back yelling at us for not cleaning the kitchen thoroughly. Her biggest pet peeve was that we didn't clean the sides of the sink and what did we use to clean. We should have used Clorox because now the edges were turning yellow. We apparently didn't do anything as well as she did. Today, she tries to wash her own dishes, but I end up rewashing them because there is still food stuck to them. I don't tell her, I just do it and put them away discreetly. The tables are now turned, and I remind her about those long past years!

After a couple of weeks, I assigned Cecilia two caregiving nights, and I was left with one night. This gave me some evening relief time to make up from the day tasks. Then if my brothers can't take a night for some reason, I'm the default for that night. By the time I get home from Mom's, I am exhausted and all I can do to release the tension is to tell Ralph about everything that happened during the day. Sometimes I just go into my peaceful craft room to start or finish a project. "Be patient," he tells me each time. It's becoming my mantra.

Tía Fina had to deal with Mom's stubbornness and now it was our turn. After weeks of Tía Fina's absence, I became more frustrated and exhausted. Laura and I have each other to vent to. She will send me a long text and finish it with, "Thank you for letting me vent." Or I will text asking if she has time to talk. If she does, I dial her and start blurting the day's frustrations and then thank her for letting me vent. When Ralph and I go to the theatre with my sister Ana, she and her husband get to hear me vent. It wasn't so bad later after I talked myself into keeping most of it in, only to hurt myself physically, as I learned later. *"Tía Fina must have badly needed her rest after dealing with Mom for two years."* Those were my first thoughts when she left for what felt like eternity, but they were only months!

The Bed Couch

"Mamá doesn't like her bed.
The new bed doesn't like her.
The new mattress kicked her out of bed.
She sleeps on the couch.
She is all twisted.
We can't put her in bed."
– Sylvia R. Merino

One of the most interesting things is that Mom refuses to sleep on her bed, and we don't understand why. Jerry, my brother, bought her a new mattress. She slept on it for a week but then she would end up on the couch. She said it hurt her back. Then she asked me to buy her a lower bed. I thought maybe she was afraid of falling again and that was the real reason for her not liking the other two mattresses. We bought her a new twin size bed and it was much lower than the other two beds. I was excited that she would sleep on this new bed. Nope! She did not like it. I tease her that she is like *The Princess and the Pea*. I bought her numerous pillows, one to prop her neck up since she has a

41

hunched back, one to put under her feet to keep them elevated since her feet swell. We even tell her that she has spent too much money on mattresses and a new bed, but she doesn't care.

For more than two years now, Mom has slept on the couch. I mentioned it to her doctor when she first began this game. I call it a game because sometimes I think she likes to test me. She is also on quarterly Prolia shots to help strengthen her bones and to prevent them from breaking. The doctor thought that after a year of Prolia her back would feel better and she would return to sleeping on the bed. That didn't happen.

Pet Peeves

"Mamá is not easy. She won't eat.
She doesn't like it. She thinks it's too sweet,
too dry, too mushy, too hard. What does she eat?
She's not tiny. She's round and short. Is the
food stuffed in her belly from long ago,
when she cooked for Papá? Or was it the food
she ate when I wasn't looking."
– Sylvia R. Merino

When Tía Fina announces that she must leave for Mexico for a doctor appointment, I instantly get a rush of stomach pangs. The pangs are from anxiety because I know that "my" life will not exist during the time she is away. I know this from the first time she left us.

I saw a naturopathic doctor to see if she could help me lower my cholesterol and fatty liver. During exams and blood work she also determined I have a weak kidney. She had me go through a few acupuncture sessions only to tell me later that my issues stem from anger. She asked what was making me angry.

She really surprised me. I mentioned having to care for Mom. I was embarrassed to tell her. Her response was to seek help from my siblings or professional caregivers. It was too much for me to explain our situation and the only relief would be to have some outsider help us with Mom. Fortunately, after a few supplements and losing 20 pounds, my liver and my cholesterol improved and so did my A1C which surprised my primary doctor. There wasn't a supplement for dealing with Mom's pet peeves, so it was left up to me to suck it up and continue to *try* to be a good caregiver.

There are many things Mom says or does that triggers a reaction, good or bad. The very first one that comes to mind is Mom's eating habits. I mentioned in prior chapters that she is a fussy eater. That is okay, because many people are. Mom just refuses to try anything new or at least taste what people bring her. They either spent money on it, or they spent hours cooking for her.

Then there's her kitchen. She leaves food on the counter all day. The butter is melted, or the unwrapped cheese is now soft. She thinks I am being a clean freak when I take the food from the counter and put it back into the refrigerator. Her mentality is that in Mexico growing up they didn't own a refrigerator and so they left their food out. Then I counter by telling her that back then, they milked the cows in the morning and drank the milk immediately and any leftover, they made cottage cheese or cheese and consumed it by the evening or sold it to the neighbors. They didn't use preservatives and so their dairy products probably did last a little longer outside of a refrigerator, especially the eggs. Then the vegetables were all fresh from the farms and they cut and cooked only what they ate for their daily meals. She has leftover chicken in the toaster oven. I ask her, "How long has the chicken been sitting in the oven?"

"Esta tapada, allí no se pierde." It's covered and, in the oven, it won't get bad, she'll tell me. I explain that the oven isn't on, so it's just like leaving it out on the counter. I grab a piece of foil and wrap it up and into the refrigerator it goes. Mom is offended but it is something she doesn't understand.

On one of the times that I took her into urgent care for a UTI, the doctor called me a day later to explain that after further testing, they discovered E.coli, a bacteria associated with food poisoning, mainly beef. Now this was a perfect opportunity to explain to Mom the danger of leaving food out of the refrigerator. When Laura buys her a hamburger, she'll eat half and saves the other half for dinner but leaves it on the counter. It's bad enough that the restaurant may have left the meat slightly raw, or they may have had it out longer than we know. She stopped eating anything with ground beef for a while. I use ground bison and so she would eat my tacos or whatever contains ground bison. As of this writing, she is now back to eating ground beef, but very little. Laura makes her shredded beef tacos. She loves those!

Secondly, as noted earlier, she fights with leftovers. She won't eat them unless it's something she REALLY likes, which is rare. I have taken her enough food for two meals. When I look in her refrigerator two or more days later, I find the leftover food untouched plus it's either half covered or completely uncovered. If my sisters take her food on one of the other days, then I will find multiple containers and soon I lose track of what's good and what's bad and everything gets thrown away. The exception is that Tía Amelia will eat her leftovers or take them to her house to eat later. That's only if she happens to be visiting before I get into Mom's refrigerator.

To avoid all these leftovers, Laura and I try to find food she likes. It was quite humorous one week when I took her barbecued ribs, corn, and the smallest deli container they had of coleslaw. She likes corn and the ribs looked delicious, so I bought myself some, too. When I walked into Mom's house, she immediately got up to see what I brought for lunch. I immediately saw her wrinkle her nose when she saw the ribs. I ignored her and went on to make a plate for her. She slowly ate what I put on her plate. I gave her two of the smallest ribs. Well, she ate all the corn and a tiny bite of one of the ribs. She told me they were too sweet. I took all the ribs home and had them for dinner! The next day, Laura offered to bring her food. "What are you craving? What would you like for dinner?" Laura asked her. "Lo que sea," Mom replies, saying "whatever." Laura playfully tells her she doesn't know where they sell "lo que sea" to make a point that she can't read her mind, so she goes to Basha's and brings her back barbecued ribs. She texted me shortly after to express her disappointment that Mom didn't like what she took her for dinner. She then proceeded to tell me she had taken her the ribs. We got on the phone, and we didn't know whether to complain or laugh. It was so coincidental that we both had the same thought to buy Mom the ribs and she turned us both down. We couldn't stop laughing.

On another day, I was pondering what to take her for dinner. I decided to take her a piece of grilled meat and a yam with all the toppings that she loves. I also took Mexican corn with green chile. When I walked in with the food, she immediately got off her chair and made her way into the kitchen to see what I brought her. I asked her if she wanted me to make her a plate.

"I'm not hungry," she tells me. "Then I'll go water the plants," I reply.

I'm somewhat annoyed with her. I water the plants praying I cool off before I go back into the house. It was only about 15 minutes later when I had the thought that either she ate junk before I got there, or she had a late lunch. I felt somewhat calmer so I went in to see if I could serve her a plate, giving it one more try. I walk in and find her eating the last bit of the yam. I asked if she even touched the meat, and she says she's not hungry. Oh, my gosh! I don't get her. She wasn't hungry when I first got to her house but within 15 minutes of me going outside, she was able to wobble her way back into the kitchen to take the yam and eat it. I feel the anger growing inside me, but instead I sigh, and I explain that I went out of my way to make her a special dinner and she didn't appreciate it. I also explained that in my household, I don't cook something new every day. We have leftovers. Yes, we'll have it for lunch the next day or have it for dinner. I don't eat breakfast, my lunch is a breakfast dish, and my dinner is the leftover. The next day could be a new dish.

So, on this day, I go home and vent to Ralph and he tells me, "You need to be patient. It's going to get worse." He knows, so I must calm down.

On another occasion, it was one of those intolerable weeks when I was already tired and needed to get some of my paintings done. They were the bottles for the church's Christmas craft event, and I felt an urgent need to finish them. So, it is my turn to stay at Mom's house for the night. I get to her house shortly after six and it's dark. She had eaten menudo that Laura had taken her earlier in the day. I went straight to the back door to go water the porch plants. When I stepped out, I almost slipped and couldn't figure out what it was. When I could finally see what I had stepped on, I could hear Mom laughing. I was stepping on menudo. My immediate thought was, *"How could she do this? Why did she deliberately throw the menudo right outside the door? That is so unlike her. Is she going crazy on me?"* She is still laughing. Any other day, watching her stomach going up and down as she laughs, would have set me off into laughter, but not this time. I shut the glass door and dragged a hose to wash the porch. I watered the plants and prayed for patience and kept breathing in and out to calm down. I was still so uptight when I went inside and more so when I see her standing at the door continuing her laughter. I went straight into the room I sleep in. She sat down and kept watching her programs on TV. It was better for me to keep silent and stay away from her.

Much later, I came out of the room and went straight into her kitchen to wash dishes and clean up more menudo mess on the floor and counters. On my way back into the room, I tell her to let me know when she's ready to go to bed (couch) so I can turn the light off. I waited and waited but she never called me to turn the lights off, and soon the room went dark. So, she turned the lights off and walked her way back to the couch in the dark. That was one more thing to tick me off. In the morning when we are both calm, she mentions that while eating the menudo at her recliner, the bowl tipped over, so she grabbed her dress and walked over to the closest place to dump it, the back porch. I told her she could have at least warned me. I then mentioned that she could have hurt herself for walking in the dark after she turned the lights off instead of calling me to do it for her.

Many days or weeks later we talk about this incident, and we laugh about it as she gives more detail on her dilemma. Since the menudo fell onto her dress, she had to keep her dress up with one hand and held the bowl with the remaining menudo holding the other end of her dress up with the other hand to keep the menudo from falling onto the carpet and floor. In other words, she created a cradle with her dress to keep the mess in. Since she walks slowly because of the surgery and didn't have a third hand to use her cane, she looked for the closest place to dump the menudo. She couldn't walk outside; the easiest thing was to dump it right outside the glass door leading to the backyard. She tells me I didn't let her explain and I tell her because I was so angry and was trying so hard not to lash out at her and the reason why I was staying out of her sight. Everything was fine after this discussion and as usual, she laughed again, thinking of my reaction when I stepped on the menudo. This time I laughed with her.

Mom does odd things. One night when one of my brothers spent the night with her, he experienced what I thought Mom was doing just when I stayed with her. Mom has the habit of leaving the stove light on all day. This night, she asks Stephen to turn the light off, and he does. Within a few minutes, Mom gets up to check that he had turned the light off. She literally goes through the trouble of getting up to check. Of course, this confuses Stephen. He mentioned this to me and so I told him that when I lock all the doors before, we settle for bed, Mom goes through the trouble of standing up to go check the locks. Stephen's reaction is much nicer than mine. I will ask, "Don't you believe me? Do you really need to get up to check?" but then I add, "Next time I won't lock them, so you have a real purpose for getting up to check them." But, of course, I lock up and she still checks. *"She needs the walk anyway,"* I tell myself.

Mom wants her independence. She wants to continue doing everything she did on her own. We allow her to do so much for herself, if it is safe. I am sure that pleases her.

The Warning Causes a Domino Effect

"Mamá is dying. That's what the
Walgreen's warnings tell her. That paper
that comes with her pills.
She believes it. It causes a visit and
another visit to the doctor. Mamá is alive and well.
She still thinks she's dying."
– Sylvia R. Merino

Mom never reads the prescription warnings that come with her medicines. One day she tells Laura that she is not taking a medicine because it was hurting her head, and her chest was pounding, and she was afraid she was close to having a stroke. Laura texted me this information and I chuckled. When I went over to check on her that same afternoon, she repeated what she told Laura. I took the document that was unfolded on the coffee table. Mom looked very worried. It was her blood pressure

50

medicine that she's taken for years, like 30+ years! I told her she would have died by now if it was true she was having all those symptoms. I Googled all her other medicines and showed her that each one had similar warnings and that she has been taking the same medicines for years. That seemed to relax her, for the time being.

Mom continued complaining about her chest, not being able to breathe. She complained about her stomach. She said the pain was moving to her side. We kept telling her it was the hernia and because she wasn't taking the medicine the gastroenterologist prescribed. One night she literally thought she was going to die from the pain. This is because a friend of hers told her that another friend had recently died of stomach cancer.

To appease Mom, I asked her if she wanted to see the doctor. I warned her that this will trigger many appointments with specialists. Sure enough, the first place she was sent to was for an ultrasound of her stomach. Nothing found except too much acid. The same thing they found from the colonoscopy and the last hospital visit.

Then she was complaining of a sore throat. A persistent sore throat she's had for over a year. The doctor had already checked for infections, and nothing was found. So, this time, she was sent to an Ear, Nose, and Throat specialist. Since she was going for the throat test, they did the hearing test. Again, nothing was found. The sore throat is dryness from not drinking enough water and aging issues, we were told. The doctor recommended throat sprays but she was never given a specific brand.

For her chest and breathing issues, she was sent to the Heart and Lung specialist. This was a bad experience, to say the least. It was also while I was still working. I take her to her first appointment, and we wait for two hours before she is called in. I thought they had forgotten her until another patient saw my worried face and told me they also had been waiting for over two hours. Once in, the doctor gives her a list of things she needs to do. The first was a lung test. The second would be an overnight test to check for sleep apnea. They couldn't do the lung test that day. The test was just walking up and down a corridor. I had to make a special appointment for this test. I also had to pick up the overnight apnea kit at another location but needed to make an appointment to pick it up. I picked up the apnea test kit a couple days later. I hooked her up to the kit that night. She had sensor tubes that went in the opening of her nostrils and the same cord had an apparatus that went around one finger, and the remaining cord was plugged into her cell phone. It was to record her breathing and heartbeat. Turns out that it failed because the tubes came out of her nose during the night. I had to reorder the test kit and this time I taped the tubes to her nose. It was a success.

The lung test went quicker. She was asked to walk back and forth for about 30 minutes on a long corridor attached to the clinic. She passed this test. Her lungs were fine. Next came the appointment with the Lung and Heart specialist to discuss the test results from both the apnea and lung test. I could not leave work, so Cecilia took Mom to this follow-up appointment. He wasn't satisfied with the apnea results. This is where communication got worse. Cecilia, along with the receptionist, were trying to reach me to set up an appointment at a sleep center to do an overnight test. I was on a conference call so I couldn't pick up the phone. Cecilia called me later in the evening to tell me what they needed and that they would call me later. I waited one day and began calling them after not hearing from them. It took many tries before I received an answer. When I explained to the receptionist that I was returning their call, the receptionist said she would have the lady who schedules appointments call me back. I never heard from her. My husband and I are getting ready to go on a trip. It was Thursday and their office is closed on Fridays. When I finally reached them, they had no clue why I was calling and said they would talk to the doctor to find out why Mom needed an appointment and would call me right back. By now it was late Thursday and still no call, so I called and left them a message to forget the call because apparently, they didn't know what they were doing. That was not nice of me, but it was true.

After this experience, I called Mom's primary doctor who referred her to this specialist, and I explained our experience, including the rude message I left on their recorder. She told me she would have done the same plus more. All her patients apparently had the same experience. I suggested we start over with a different doctor at a different location but by then Mom was feeling worse and was getting impatient with doctors. We eventually repeated the apnea test at a different location, and it was determined that Mom has a healthy heart. The shortness of breath she was feeling is because she doesn't walk enough. She sits all day knitting and watching her shows.

Mom's PA was not as personable or as knowledgeable about Mom's history, and it was getting worse each time we went in for follow-ups or annual checkups. She just wasn't as thorough as the doctor my sister and brother-in-law and I see. We really like our doctor, but she was not taking new patients. I thought it wouldn't hurt to ask, so I asked. Our doctor was thrilled to take Mom on as a new patient. She immediately started with a wellness checkup. We had all her prior doctor's records transferred. Her medication history was also loaded to the new doctor's medical portal. This reminds me of the day that the doctor began using the portal and she was complaining that she had to retype data from one location to the other. I then chimed in and said, "Just copy and paste." Every so often she'll tell me how much time I saved her.

At Mom's second appointment, I asked her to tell the doctor about all her symptoms. I had to intervene when she mentioned her stomach aches. I explained to the doctor that Mom had a colonoscopy not too long ago and that she also had the stomach ultrasound, and I explained the hiatal hernia and that she won't take the omeprazole regularly. She takes a thyroid medicine first thing in the morning and can't eat for 30 minutes after taking it. The omeprazole instructions also indicate not to eat a meal until after 30 minutes of taking it. Mom was so confused, so the doctor decided that Mom could take both the omeprazole and the thyroid medicine together since they worked on different parts of the body. This helped. She couldn't refer Mom anywhere else since she had seen most specialists. It was just a matter of keeping watch and doing lab work to ensure Mom was not going downhill.

The exception is the swelling of her feet and her continued complaints of her chest pounding. Knowing Mom's history, Laura and I get together and talk about what we really think is going on in Mom's mind. We truly think it's anxiety issues, thinking she's going to die from the medicines she's taking. Thanks to the medicine brochures with the warnings.

Mom's feet sometimes turn beet red. She is diabetic, so there is a fear of heart issues and neuropathy. She has been told to keep her feet elevated when she's sitting and in bed (couch) to keep them propped up on a pillow AND drink lots of water. Mom, like many elderly people, does not drink enough water. Mom says it is because she'll need to go to the restroom frequently. So, Mom was referred to a cardiologist.

The cardiologist ordered a cardiography (Echo), a stress test, and an angiography to see if her blood is flowing normally and to make sure her heart is well. I took her for the three tests. They were split between two days. On both days, we check in and wait in the emergency lobby for an hour. Then she is called into a small office to sign agreements and to be presented with her bill. All tests total over $6K but fortunately, her insurance that is not Medicare covers most of it. We then get directed to a second waiting room and wait another 40 minutes. A lab technician takes her in a wheelchair. Thank goodness, otherwise, it would have taken another 30 minutes to get to the lab, walking at her pace.

The Echo and the nuclear medicine stress tests were done on the first day. For the stress test, she was told to take a snack. I didn't understand why, but I know now. They performed the stress test first. Mom said it was the worst thing ever and that she would rather die than to go for a second one. She came out shaking and looked like she had jogged miles. I gave her the snack. We had about 45 minutes to an hour before she was called in for the Echo. The next morning, we went in for the angiography.

This one went much easier. Everyone at the hospital were very nice and made it comfortable for her.

After all this, everything was normal except for a small calcification in one of the arteries of her left leg. The cardiologist said it was not anything to worry about. As we leave the doctor's clinic, he tells all the nurses, "Look at this 90-year-old woman who looks like she's in her seventies." Mom has no wrinkles on her face, all natural. Mom is clueless about what all the noise is that's about her. She gets in the car and sits silently. She has a worried look. As I turned into her driveway, she exclaims, "Well, I still have all the pains. So, what did the tests and doctor do for me?" I feel badly for her. I interpret what the doctor told the staff about her looking so young to try to cheer her up. It makes me sad and guilty that I can't make her feel well. If the doctors can't, how can I? The thing is that Mom can help relieve some of her pains by obeying the doctor's orders. I carry the sadness home and the only thing I can do is wait for the next event.

Later, Laura and I, as we are overwhelmed with our personal lives, discover that Mom was not taking her antidepressant. The doctor discovered it during one of Mom's visits. It was on the list from her previous doctor's records, yet it was marked as "not taking, remove." The doctor asked, "Who authorized she stop taking it?"

"Mom did, I really don't know." I answered, quite confused and horrified. We are both confused. She tells me to check with Laura as she knows Laura takes care of Mom's pills. The doctor asks I communicate with her through the portal. She will refill the medicine if she was taking it.

I go home concerned that we've been depriving Mom of one of her medicines. Laura checks her list and finds it but doesn't remember if she's been giving it to Mom. We are both scratching our head. Laura then remembers trying to refill it, but it was never refilled. I tell the doctor that she needs it refilled, but I am hesitant. I can hear Mom telling me a few years back, that her PA told her she could stop taking it. Her current doctor said it would be dangerous if she was supposed to be taking it and hasn't been taking it. It would mean that it will take about six weeks for the medicine to take effect. She asked if Mom was depressed. I didn't think so, but then I started seeing strange behavior, or I was just thinking it. By this time, Laura and I are so worried that we were messing with Mom's health or had already messed it up.

We finally decided that Mom should be taking it. Her doctor sent in a prescription. When Laura was putting her pills in her pill box a few days later, she found an old half empty bottle of the antidepressant pills that she used to put in her box. She went back to her texts, way back, like a year back. She discovered a text from me that said she needed to fill the prescription or something to that effect. So, Mom was taking it but then later, Mom told us to stop them per the PA's instructions. It was around the time we had moved her to her new doctor. Even though we couldn't tell she was going into depression when the doctor questioned us, but after taking the antidepressants for a few weeks, she looked better, happier, and more like herself.

This confusing incident gave us a big scare. Personally, I felt very responsible for the mix-up. The doctor told me it happens. We get too involved with everyday activities and on top of it, we are trying to keep up with Mom's health, life, and comfort.

Mother of All Saints

"Too much to see. Mamá
sits and sits. Saints look at me.
Wall pictures talk to me. What are
they saying? Too many speak.
I don't understand. The kitchen calls me.
It's too small but they all fit,
squished, but we all fit."
– Sylvia R. Merino

Walking into Mom's home, you see her sitting in her recliner staring at the TV blasting the afternoon *Doctora* (Judge show) or if it's 2:30 or 3:30 depending on the program's time zone, she will be watching EWTN (Eternal World Television Network, a Catholic station) and praying the rosary. At 4:30 she's on Telemundo watching the news. I observe that the Mexican news seem to be more updated than the U.S. news.

On one side of the recliner, she has a small table that was supposed to be for her small medicine dish and her glass and one remote control. Instead, Mom keeps a small plate with sewing needles of different sizes, and outside of the dish there are numerous knitting and crochet needles and two pair of scissors of the same size. She has two remote controls and her cell phone. Something is always falling off the table. Underneath the table, she has other items, one being her big pill box that is always half hanging off the shelf. The glass coffee table has all her knitting yarn, and a pile of prayer and saint books. Then there's the antique phone book with phone numbers, mostly of friends who have passed away. On the front cover she has scribbled a few phone numbers of friends still living. Tucked inside are the prayer cards from funerals. Another pile is mail she accumulates. It's mail from organizations asking for donations. I caution Mom that she will go broke if she begins donating to every organization that sends her mail. Today, she doesn't write checks so when she asks us to write a check to one of these organizations, we make sure it's legit or it's a one-time donation.

Then my eyes move onto the walls and shelves. There are statues on the shelves and fireplace mantel. There are pictures of saints and crosses on the walls. There are at least 50 pictures of her children, grandchildren, and her great-grandchildren on her walls and shelves mixed in with the statues. The only organized wall is the wall where our father's military picture and the flag that is encased in a shadow box hang. It is the only thing on that wall.

There's a sofa table to the side, not visible until you enter the living room. On top, there are more pictures, but off to the side there are at least five bottles of lotion. There was also a bottle of sanitizer that I caught Mom using a few times. Because of Mom's eye problems, I told her that if she touches her eyes after using the sanitizer, it could sting her eyes. I know that just the smell makes my eyes burn. I also explained that sanitizers are convenient when outside of the house. "Use the soap in the bathroom to wash your hands." I tell her. I finally removed the sanitizer from the table so that she wouldn't be tempted to keep using it.

All these odds and ends in her living area are for convenient purposes. Since she can barely walk, it is easier to have the lotion close by. All her yarns kept on the coffee table, I finally put them in a basket. Tía Fina stores the yarn she's not using. I've offered to put some of her books away, but she says, "No, I read them all at one time or another, plus I won't find them if you hide them." She thinks that putting things away where they belong is like hiding them.

I wonder, *"Do all elderly people live like Mom or is it only our Mom who has these odd organization skills?"* Dad was the organizer in our family. Mom has always been messy but clean. In other words, she didn't like a dirty kitchen sink or counter, but she would leave things out on the counter instead of putting them away. These are little things that still irritate me. I'm more like Dad, always picking up things, cleaning to the point that people would say they could eat off my floors, especially when we had our wooden floors in Colorado.

Tía Fina is very organized, maybe too organized, and sometimes that worries me. She puts everything in the kitchen in the cabinets, either below or in the top cabinets. Mom is short and she can't reach up high, and she can't bend down. If she bends, she falls forward. She can't balance herself. I'm fine with food hidden when Tía Fina is there because she can take things out for Mom. When Tía Fina leaves for Rayón, I take things out. For example, there is a small microwavable dish she likes to use for small lunches and a bowl that I pull out from hiding and leave on the counter. Then she likes honey, but she can't get to it, so that also goes back on the counter. Her snacks are also put back on the counter. In the living room, I put out more yarn in case Mom wants to knit something different from what she was knitting before Tía Fina left. It must irritate Tía Fina when she gets back, having to put everything back where she had it!

Mom is afraid to walk into any of the rooms that are carpeted because she says the cane gets stuck and she's afraid she'll fall. Her closet is in one of these rooms so rather than having Tía Fina bring her a dress to wear, I thought Mom would like to choose her own dress. So, to make it more convenient for Mom, I bought her a clothes rack and put it in her sewing room. The room is big and has lots of space for the rack. I hung her everyday dresses on one side and her nicer dresses on the other side, and her super nice dresses remain in her closet. She had her dresses on those ugly wire hangers, so I bought her good hangers. She scolded me that I was wasting money on things she didn't need. I ignore her. To her delight, she is now able to choose her dress (and nightgown). I still find the dresses lying on the bed and not on a hanger and that annoys me! Oh well, *"be patient,"* I tell myself.

Mom has so many clothes that don't fit her anymore or are no longer in style. She won't let me get rid of them so sometimes I sneak one or two tops and take them home and put them in a giveaway box. She has never asked about them. She forgot she had them.

I also found a bag of my daughter's clothes that I had given her to send to Rayón years ago. They were in the back of our dad's closet. I was looking for a box of pictures when I ran into the bag. Mom said she was saving it for someone from church but forgot about them. They eventually did go to Rayón. I also stopped giving her boxes of my clothes because she tried wearing them. They weren't appropriate for her. They were short blouses and looked funny on her with her belly almost hanging out. She rarely wears slacks now, so she rarely wears blouses unless it's cold when I take her to a doctor appointment. She has a separate set of clothes for those occasions. She tells me I worry too much about how she looks . . . maybe I do.

Aside from what we see upon entering our mom's home, we are hit with the aroma of freshly made tortillas or the smell of beans cooking in a big stock pot. Sometimes the smell is as if something has burned. It is not a mistake to have an almost burnt tortilla. Mom loves to toast her tortillas to have with her egg in the morning. These are small round tortillas my Tía Fina makes from scratch. For Mom's green chile and cheese burritos she uses pieces of a large tortilla Tía Fina brings from Rayón. These are tortillas that are paper thin, and the size is about 14 inches in diameter. I've made mini chimichangas with these tortillas. One tortilla will make at least four to six chimichangas depending on the size. Of course, you can use the whole tortilla to make a Chipotle size burrito.

Back to Mom's home. Whether Mom is alone or Tía Fina is there, when she knows we are bringing food, she quickly jumps out of her recliner when she sees us walk into her home. She follows us into her small kitchen. If Tía Fina is cooking and I am unloading groceries or prepared food, Mom has a habit of standing right in the middle of the kitchen hovering over us. We tell her that one day she will get knocked out or one of us will. That's exactly what happened to Tía Amelia when she was also trying to get into the kitchen. When Mom turned to go back to her recliner, not knowing Tía Amelia was behind her she moved her cane at the same time Tía Amelia stepped into the kitchen and ended up getting tangled on Mom's cane. She fell hard on her back, slid across the room, landing against the couch. I held Mom from falling with her. This incident didn't stop Mom from crowding the kitchen. When Laura refills Mom's pill box, Mom stands right next to her, annoying Laura every second. Not only are we caring for Mom but for my two Tías. It is sad when we think that there are only three ladies left from a family of seven siblings. We want to keep them as long as we can, antics and all!

Thinking back to this incident, I think about how irritated I sometimes get with Mom. Is it because she is my Mom? When I would take my mother-in-law to a doctor appointment or to a massage or even just shopping, I would never feel irritated. The only thing is that she walked so slow and couldn't hear. She refused to wear her hearing aids. When I returned home from those rare trips I would go for a fast walk or just move around the house doing things to get that locked-up energy out of my system.

With Mom, I think it's because Mom wants to do things her way, and I want her to do it my way. It's a tug-of-war. When I was younger growing up, it was always her way. I didn't have a say-so in anything I wanted to do. After school, after completing my homework, or on a weekend after chores, I would sit down to read or draw or to sew clothes for my dolls, she would always, without fail, call me to do something for her. It was either to find something she lost, and she would always say that I always found lost items as if that was a motivator. Even now as adults, I'm always waiting for her to ask me to do something the minute I sit down.

At my mother-in-law's it was a time to rest or play. We spent time working on puzzles or played Chinese checkers. If we had dinner, I always helped wash dishes but knew that shortly after we would sit and talk or continue finding the pieces needed to complete a puzzle.

On rare occasions, Mom would sit with me to teach me how to sew but if I made one mistake, she had me undo everything and restart. I hated that part. Later, I mastered the hand-made sewing of the "Barbie" dresses, but they were really Midge and Tammy dolls. We didn't have Barbie dolls until much later. I used all the left-over pieces of the brides' dresses and the colorful bridesmaid dresses or the quinceañera dresses she sewed for friends.

These are dresses I made for Melissa's Barbie dolls.

62

In Mom's current sewing room, she has her machine out ready to use. She has cabinets with drawers filled with leftover ribbons, buttons, patterns, and lots of thread of different colors. It is sad to see this picture because that is all that is left, just a frozen picture. She hasn't touched anything in that room in more than a year, other than her clothes.

Moving on to the rest of the house. She has statues on dressers and crosses and saint pictures hanging on each wall in every room. You would think that when walking through this house I would be a saintly daughter but sometimes I feel more like a possessed creature. Well, not really that bad!

So, this is Mom's home. It is cozy. The great-grandchildren think it is the biggest playroom. They go in and out of the rooms. We have left a small basket with stuffed animals, so the kids have something to play with. The older girls love to play store. They bring out whatever they find in the closets and from Mom's sewing room and "sell" the items between themselves. I do need to say that Mom in her older age looks forward to seeing her great-grandchildren. She was always too busy to appreciate the grandchildren. Of course, that's when she was healthier and very busy with her sewing and doing everything a housewife and mother had to do.

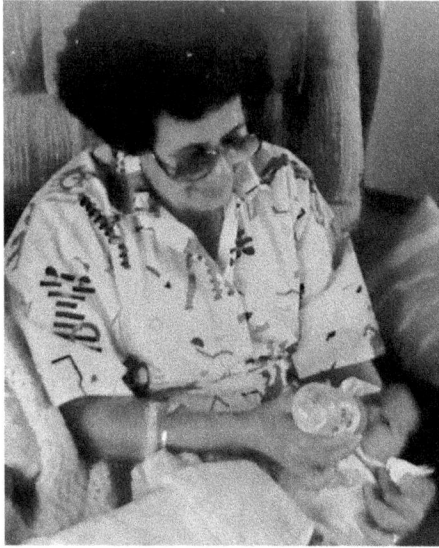

Mom feeding Melissa, at one week old.

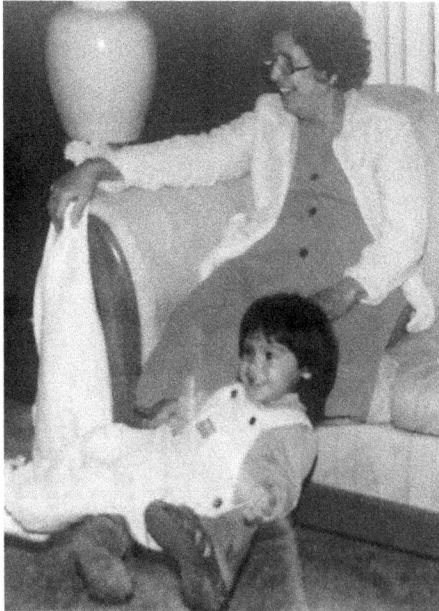

Mom had more quality time with my daughter. This is mainly
because we didn't live in Tucson, so she took advantage of
the short periods she got to see her.

Mom's 90th birthday party was a memorable one. We created an album with pictures of each grandchild. Each one wrote a memory. In the top picture, they are showing Mom a funny entry by my nephew, David (standing to the right).

Mom wasn't as playful with us, as she is with the grandchildren, and the reason I love this picture. She is loving the attention.

65

Unstable But Trying

"Mamá don't walk on grass.
She does, she slips. She falls, falls
way down. Too heavy, I pull up, up.
She's up. She walks. She sits. I hurt.
I'm quiet, she's quiet.
We are not broken."
– Sylvia R. Merino

I'm beginning to think that I am praying the Stations of the Cross. This is a Catholic Lenten prayer. There are 14 Stations of the Cross. They are from the time that Jesus is condemned until He is laid in the tomb. Three of them count each time He has fallen carrying the cross throughout his painful journey. So, this is Mom's third fall.

Shortly after the menudo incident, in mid-June of 2023, it was one of those days that Tía Fina was gone for a couple of weeks. It was my turn to spend the night. I am outside watering the plants. When it's over 100 degrees, we also water the big fig, lemon, grapefruit, and orange trees with the hose even if they are watered earlier in the morning with the drip system. I am out by the fig tree that is at the far east corner of Mom's backyard. Mom is getting around just fine with her cane. My poor Mom wants so much to do things that she loved to do years ago, but she now has limitations. We know she can walk outside if she's careful. Normally, she will sit on the porch on a metal chair and watch me water. This day, I see her stepping onto the grass. The grass is high. Jerry, my brother, normally does the yard work, and it was time for him to mow the lawn. When I saw Mom stepping onto the grass, I tried to stop her, "Don't walk on the grass, you will trip," I called out. Within seconds, she fell on her stomach. Fortunately, she didn't land on the brick pavers.

Mom is moaning and asking me to call Delbert, my brother-in-law, to pick her up. I tell her, "I will pick you up, but you need to help me." I knew she wasn't injured, just sore. So, I bent down carefully so as not to hurt my back. By this time, she is on her hands and knees, so it was easy for me to put my arms around her in a way that she could use my body to hang onto. She was not budging. I told her again to help me a little bit by pushing her feet to stand. Miraculously, she finally stands. My back is burning and so are my knees, but I can't think about me. I walk her to the porch and help her walk back and forth along the length of the porch and at the end I help her sit on a chair. "Do you want to go to emergency?" I asked. She tells me that she didn't break anything and is only sore. We go inside and I give her water and Advil.

She continued to complain about being sore. Her back hurt and now her thighs were hurting. She already had an appointment set up with her primary doctor, and it was only three days away. My husband and I were also leaving to go on vacation the following week. I was concerned that perhaps she had fractured her lower back. She walked slower than usual. She asked for her rollator walker that she refused to use so I knew she was very afraid of falling again. She prefers the rollator because it is smaller than the typical wider walker, and fits through the bathroom door. It also has a seat with storage underneath it. Sometimes she uses it to carry small items from room to room.

I took her to her doctor's appointment. It was a Wednesday, and we were to leave for Colorado the following Friday. After the doctor finished with the regular exam, I mentioned Mom's fall. I also mentioned that she refused to go to the hospital. Mom screamed when the doctor touched her stomach around the location Mom pointed to where she felt discomfort. The doctor suggested an X-ray to be sure she didn't fracture her back or pelvic bone. It was late in the day, and we had one hour to get the X-ray scheduled. I had parked the car close to the clinic and the lab is directly across from the clinic. The doctor was able to get Mom's appointment for that same afternoon; in fact, she was the last patient that day.

When we walked outside, I turned to go into the car, but Mom says, "I can walk. Just walk slowly."

"Are you sure?" I asked. She confirmed she needed to walk. So, we made a game out of this short walk. She is clinging onto me with one arm, with her cane in the other. We looked like the characters in Wizard of Oz as we counted the steps from the clinic to the lab. It was exactly 67 steps. Mom looked tired but didn't say a thing. She was immediately taken into the X-ray room. I helped her get into the gown and to get her on the bed. Mom can't ever pull herself up to the pillow nor can she scoot to the middle. I don't have the strength to move her around and usually the nurses don't either, so I help the nurse and technician get her into the position needed for the X-ray or whatever procedure she is having. On the way out, Mom quietly asks, "Would you bring the car over?" She was tired and didn't want to walk 67 steps back to the car! That was fair.

It was confirmed that she didn't fracture anything. She must have just been bruised internally. There were no bruises on her body that I could see. Her doctor was still concerned, though, and asked me to have Laura continue to check on her pain. If the pain was persistent or was more intense Laura was to notify her and she would order an MRI. While we were in Colorado,

I checked in a few times and was told she was fine. The pain finally went away but she was left with a slower walk and her legs continue to give her problems.

My husband and I left for Colorado, concerned about leaving Mom alone during the day. Laura would surely check on her, but I thought she would need more assistance. Mom, being stubborn, told us she was fine. So, there was nothing more I could do.

On occasion, we have found a bowl and fork on the floor. Mom had dropped it and because she can't bend down, it stayed on the floor. Another time, Laura found water on the floor and a broken glass under the kitchen counter. One day, I walked in and on the chest in the entryway the container that I had brought earlier with pineapple slices was sitting there empty with the fork outside of the container. It is beyond me as to why she was eating while walking.

Our Tía Fina returned just a day after we left for Colorado, so that took some worry off my shoulders. When we returned, I learned that Mom can no longer pull her feet up on the couch, so she needs help. Later she decides she wants one leg dangling on the side of the couch but on a pillow. The other is on the couch somewhat elevated. It really bothers me that she won't sleep on her bed, especially when I see how she is positioned on the couch. I would be so uncomfortable, yet she tells us it's comfortable for her. How can we argue!

Knot on Forehead, Subtle Mistakes

"Mamá kneeling, head on rollator. Can't get up.
Help is called. Big man lifts her, takes her to sit.
Man asks, who is president. Mamá knows, she knows.
She is okay. She can think, she can walk, she can see.
She can knit . . . or can she?"
– Sylvia R. Merino

While we were in Colorado, there was one day Laura had to be in Phoenix to care for her grandchildren. Tía Fina had just finished helping Mom with her shower and had helped her with her dress. Mom quickly turns to grab the rollator but somehow misses the handles and falls on her knees and bangs her head on the seat. Mom can't get up. Tía Fina can't lift her. Mom tells her to call Cecilia, but not to bother Laura. Cecilia has friends over, so she wasn't called. Tía Fina finally calls Laura only to find out that Laura is out of town. Laura calls Cecilia

70

and she immediately goes to Mom's house. Cecilia can't pick her up, so they call 911. The paramedics show up. They pick her up and carry her to her recliner. Before they left, they gave her and my Tía warnings of a future fall if she didn't remove the rug that was under the coffee table and the rug right inside the front door.

Thankfully, Mom was fine after this fall. She did have a bruise on her forehead. After this incident she once again refused to use the rollator and went back to her cane.

The paramedics also pointed out the wobbly side table Mom was using. When I returned from Colorado, I immediately got rid of it and replaced it with a sturdy table with three shelves. We removed the rug that was in the entryway. We didn't remove the big carpet under the coffee table immediately.

What is odd about this fall, is that no one told me about it until I talked to my sister Ana while driving back home from Colorado. She asks, "Did anyone tell you Mom fell?" I'm like, "What?"

I was told that Mom told Laura not to tell me because she didn't want to worry me. I'm surprised she would worry about my feelings, but I am thankful I didn't know until I was on my way back home.

When I visited Mom the day after we returned from Colorado, I found her sitting in her recliner on top of three flat pillows, a pillow behind her back, and a neck roll that is now too soft. *"This reminds me that I should make her a new one."* This sitting position has been like this for quite some time. She slouches and it's the worst thing she could do for her back. She won't allow us to remove the pillows. They are comfortable enough for her. All looks good from the fall, and everything is back to normal. She is knitting a sweater for the church's Fall craft sale. She motions for me to go into the sewing room to look at the finished knitted blanket that goes with the sweater she's knitting.

When I pick up the blanket, I notice a puckered square. At further inspection, I see Mom's error. I walk back thinking, *"Oh Mom, you can't knit anymore but I can't say that so what do I say?"* I tell her that I think there's a mistake. She looks at it and

71

immediately agrees. She said she miscounted because she was watching a program on the TV and lost the count. I offered to remove the square and she gladly accepted it. She was going to knit another square to replace the bad square. I put the blanket back on the bed with the hole where the missing square will go.

A couple of days later, I went to Mom's house and sat down to talk to her. I was looking at the Blue Cross/Blue Shield envelope and then my eyes fell on a knitted square. I was assessing it, wondering if it was for a new blanket. "Are you knitting a new blanket?" I ask.

"No, that was the old square, go look at the quilt — it's all fixed."

I knew it was not fixed when I saw that the square on the table was perfectly knitted. *"Is it possible she put the bad square back on?"* I thought as I walked to the sewing room. *"Oh my gosh!"* I said quietly. Mom had put the bad square back in. I walked out to show her. She was devastated when she saw what she had done. I felt sorry for her because she is getting to the point where her knitting isn't as accurate as it used to be. She had already knitted two small sweaters that were lopsided. I took them home and fixed one with the same color of thread and needle. I don't knit so I had to mend it from the inside so it wouldn't look bad. It looked okay. The other I pressed until both sides looked even. Babies don't know that one sleeve is wider than the other!

When Mom has a knitting project in mind, she aims to finish it in one or two days. Since the day I took her a bag of donated yarn to be used for the church craft fair, she has sat knitting as fast as she can. I mentioned multiple times that she has six months to finish them. Her mind works differently. She thinks she's going to die tomorrow, and she won't get a chance to finish all that she has to do.

Mom made this one for my daughter. She wore it until she grew out of it. I saved all the sweaters mom knitted for her.

Mom knitted the top sweater about a year ago. She just found it in a drawer. The one below, she knitted it right before she turned 93 (9/11/24).

It is heart-wrenching to see our parents deteriorate. We will someday go that direction, so I try to be patient and gentle when I suggest that perhaps Tía Fina can help with the baby blankets. Tía Fina's work is as beautiful as Mom's used to be. On a good day, Mom can still knit a pretty and flawless baby sweater. On a bad day, not so good. She is 93, after all! She is doing more than just sitting watching TV. She keeps her hands busy. I just wish she would elevate her feet while she's sitting but she won't listen to me!

Mom used to make our tortillas, the Lenten *capirotada* (bread pudding), and *arroz con leche* (rice pudding). The *arroz con leche* was mainly cooked for her sons. They love it!

One day when Tía Fina was in Mexico during lent, Mom decided to make *capirotada*. She didn't ask us to buy her groceries, other than the bolillo bread (French bread). The capirotada consists of layers of bolillo bread, raisins, bananas, peanuts, cheese, cinnamon sticks, and *piloncillo* (raw brown sugar, cone shaped). I couldn't wait to taste it.

The aroma in the house smelled of burnt sugar and a mix of bitter fruit and cinnamon. The *capirotada* looked so good, I couldn't wait to try it. I served myself a plate, and at the first bite, I exclaimed, "Oh my gosh, it is too sweet, much too sweet to eat!" Mom laughed and said,

"I know, I am throwing it away." I felt so sorry for her. I asked what she put in it. Since she didn't have the *piloncillo*, she used half of a package of brown sugar and about a cup of pancake syrup. Usually, it's one piloncillo melted in a pan with a few sticks of cinnamon. I felt so bad for Mom. "Next time, call me and I'll help you." I tell her as I see her disappointment.

Another thing we struggle with is when I take her to her appointments; it is a chore getting her into the car. She won't sit before putting her legs in the car so she's constantly asking me to lift her feet into the car. Most of the time, I can't reach over her to get to her feet, and she ends up doing it herself. One day, Ralph was driving us somewhere, probably a party. We put Mom in front with him because the passenger seat is much lower than the back seats. Ralph saw her struggling and he motions for her to sit down first. I've been telling her this for years. This time, on Ralph's suggestion, she sits first and lo and behold she's able to easily put her feet in. After this, I don't need to fight with her about sitting first, although, I do need to remind her when I see her getting in the car the wrong way. I also tease her that she only listens to Ralph.

The Finger

Mamá hurries, hurries, she
can't wait. It's now, now. Bends to turn
water on. She wants it warm, warm and can't wait.
Slips, falls, falls, lands on toilet. Finger
hurts, can't move it. She gives
me the finger."
– Sylvia R. Merino

It is the end of August 2023. I was going to a finger therapist to see if they could help straighten out one of my fingers that was damaged from RA. I had weekly appointments. One day, I was in the middle of typing the manuscript for my first book and had planned to stop early to get to my therapy appointment but then I received a very early call that Mom fell. Since I couldn't take her to urgent care immediately, I stopped by the store to buy a finger brace. When I finished with my therapy, I called Mom to get ready for me to take her to urgent care. I hadn't asked how she fell. I was too focused on my manuscript and the finger therapy appointment.

First, I came home to make the appointment. Fortunately, they recognized her name and immediately told me they could see her now. I explained that I was at home and would need to go pick her up. They told me I didn't need an appointment and that they would have the paperwork ready for us. Within 45 minutes, I had Mom at the urgent care. Her finger was X-rayed, and we were told she had a small fracture. Mom wasn't complaining about the pain. The urgent care PA told me the sling I bought was fine until she saw the bone doctor.

On the way home, I finally asked how she fell. She seemed confused and couldn't clearly tell me. When we were back in her house, I asked Tía Fina what had happened. She explained that Mom got hasty with her shower and instead of letting Tía Fina reach over to turn the shower water on, she reached over, lost her balance, and fell between the toilet and the shower. She got her hand tangled on the toilet tank somehow. Since Tía Fina couldn't pick her up, Delbert and Laura were called to help. Laura was out walking early. She had her cell phone and so was able to call Delbert to meet her at Mom's house. Laura had offered to take her to urgent care but as I recall she was on her way back to Phoenix to care for her grandchildren. Since I know all of Mom's medical history, it's always best I just deal with urgent care and medical appointments.

The bone doctor didn't see Mom until the following week. In the meantime, Mom was determined to continue knitting. Her finger was getting more swollen by the day. She got tired of the finger brace and decided to not use anything until the pain was unbearable. I switched the finger brace with a gel pad that was taped around her finger. That gave her some comfort and she continued to knit. She's amazing. She complains about the pain but continues to knit even knowing that the knitting is what's causing the additional pain.

When we get to the bone doctor's clinic, she is taken in for an X-ray. Mom is always gassy. When she came back into the room, she quietly tells me that she passed gas. I was so embarrassed but she's laughing. So at least now, I felt better that she must not be in excruciating pain. The doctor confirms that she has a small fracture on her middle finger of her left hand. He wound medical tape around her middle and ring fingers, gave her a roll of tape to continue to replace it. He asked to see her in a month.

As usual, Mom sits in the car sad that he couldn't fix it right away. I explained, as the doctor did, that it will heal in time. When we get home, she tells Tía Fina that the doctor didn't do anything except put the tape around her fingers. She sat down and looked at her knitting but didn't touch it. When we get home from any doctor appointment, I remind her to wash her hands. She struggles as she gets up to wash her hands and complains that I am so *mandona*, bossy. I can see how bugged she is about the whole finger situation.

One day after the appointment with the bone doctor, I went to Mom's house to deliver something or other. Mom tells me she is keeping the tape on her finger like the doctor told her, lifting her arm to show me her wrapped finger. I look up and see she has the tape on the wrong finger. After I pointed that out, we all had a good laugh. I had to remind her and Tía Fina that the tape should go around both fingers as instructed, not just the fractured one.

Mom in the car after a doctor appointment.
She's thinking why the doctor didn't fix her pain or fractures.

Solving the Puzzle, Not With the Gummy

"Tía Fina can't sleep. Stares at ceiling. Counts
sheep. Prays 100 Hail Marys. Takes CBD's, she flies
into the clouds. All night, all night she goes
higher and higher."
– Sylvia R. Merino

A month later, Tía Fina goes back to Rayón for a doctor
appointment. This time she returns within a couple of weeks.
Something is not going well with her. She is not sleeping, and
it could cause problems caring for Mom. She has tried counting
sheep and praying — and nothing works. I know what it's like
not to be able to get a whole night's sleep. I feel badly for my tía
and wish I could do something for her but because of her kidney situation, she can't take any over-the-counter medications.
I texted Lupita to ask if I could give her a sleeping pill. She tells
me only if it is a natural pill. I find one at Sprouts and she takes

it for two nights and she's still not sleeping. Then I remembered being at a CBD store one day and an elderly man was asking questions about a CBD gummy for his wife who couldn't sleep. I texted Lupita again to ask if I could try them. She approved so I bought the smallest packet of the CBD gummies. Tía Fina hesitantly took one that night. The next day when I went to check on her and Mom, my tía tells me she was up in the clouds having dreams all night but was still in and out of her sleep. She was looking very, very tired.

"Why aren't you sleeping? What is troubling you?" I asked her. She says she forgot her anxiety pills in Mexico. Lupita and her husband went to Nogales, Sonora, that night to pick up a prescription for the pills. Before this occurred, I bought her a packet of kiwi fruit. I know that kiwi has helped my husband sleep. She ate half of one and said she slept for the first time that night but for only four hours, which was better than none. Finally, the pills came late that night.

A couple of days passed, and Tía Amelia calls me to tell me that Mom called to ask if she could buy Tía Fina something because her chest was hurting or something was. Tía Amelia gets just as nervous and anxious as they do, so she tells them that she can't drive, that she hasn't driven too far from her house since she had her fall months ago. When she calls me, she is so concerned and tells me to go buy whatever she needed. I called Mom to try to get clarification on the situation. Mom called Tía Amelia because she is a retired licensed practitioner nurse and thought she would know what over-the-counter medicine she would need. She thought even a Sprite would help if it was nausea she was feeling. Since I was told it was stomach or maybe a chest pain, and since they weren't clear where the pain was, I settled for Mylanta.

When I get to Mom's, Tía Fina still didn't look rested from all the lost sleep. She was sitting on the couch watching TV with Mom. I noticed her clenching her hands; then she would sit on them. She was so anxious. I told them how panicked Tía Amelia sounded. They tell me that she had a stomach pain, not a chest pain. Luckily, I chose the right medicine, so I gave her one medicine cup of Mylanta. I sat next to her for a few minutes. She needed to calm down. I knew her stomach had built up acid from the anxieties and from not sleeping.

We talked about her anxieties. She told me she gets them frequently and that is why they have her on medication. Later, someone recounted the many times they've witnessed her anxieties when in Rayón. They gave me the example of when her brother, my uncle Manuel, passed away, she was very young. She couldn't cry, and almost died from an anxiety attack. The ladies around her couldn't get her to breathe, but finally she came out of it. Okay, so I was relieved that she wasn't having a heart attack! Then it finally comes out, that she, too, was prescribed omeprazole for acid reflux. I felt better about giving her the second cup of the Mylanta. Everything made sense. She was totally stressing from the lack of sleep and so the acid was building up and now the Mylanta will slowly calm the acid. She looked much better, and she wasn't clasping her hands, so I left, knowing I had done the right thing.

That weekend, Lupita took her to her house for the weekend to see if she could get her to calm down and on a sleeping routine. She came back feeling much better and more rested. I love Tía Fina, and as much as she cares for Mom, I want to take care of her as well. Plus, she is my tía and don't like to see her suffering.

The Mysterious Fall

"Mamá falls, lays head on pillow, not
by choice. She can't get up. No one hears her.
She's tired, she sleeps, she waits, waits until sister
wakes up. Calls for help. I'm not told.
She's back up. How did she fall?
It's a mystery."
– Sylvia R. Merino

One day when Tía Fina left for a doctor's appointment, it was Tía Amelia's turn to spend the night with Mom. It was two in the morning when Mom fell going back to the couch. She had gotten up to use the restroom. She doesn't remember why she fell. She was found with her head on the pillow she leans one of her legs on at night. Her head was on the side of the TV, yet she sleeps on the opposite side. Then Laura said she had the TV remote in one hand. This fall is still very confusing. As Mom ages and loses her memory, it will be more difficult learning the facts when we are not present to witness her actions.

Mom falls and screams out for Tía Amelia. "Amelia, I fell, come pick me up." Tía Amelia is hard of hearing and doesn't wear her hearing aids to bed. She couldn't hear Mom's screams. At about nine the next morning, Tía Amelia comes out of her room to find Mom on the floor. Since no one can help Mom get up alone anymore, Amelia calls Laura. They literally both said to Laura, "Don't tell Sylvia." Laura and her husband go to Mom's and help her up. Thankfully, Mom wasn't hurt. My guess is that Mom must have gotten dizzy and couldn't balance herself, so she fell. This fall is still a mystery.

After this incident, we all realized we should have never had Tía Amelia be part of the night watchers. With her not wearing her hearing aids at night, that makes it dangerous, for so many reasons. What if there was a fire, or Mom was choking, or falls again. Or like the New Year's Eve night I stayed with Mom. We heard the usual noise of fireworks going off. We could ignore them, but at exactly midnight, brats were ringing her doorbell. Then five minutes later they were pounding on her garage door. I was frightened and called 911. It took 35 minutes before I heard or saw a cop. We did hear a helicopter within 10 minutes of the call and that's when the neighborhood went quiet and so did the pounding and ringing. When the cop finally came, he was passing by Mom's home apologizing for not calling sooner. He said he had called the helicopter out to the neighborhood because of all the noise and then because of my call. He also mentioned that he saw an Uber pull up, dropping off a couple on Mom's street. We think it was the kids of a new family who had just moved into her neighborhood. I suppose the kids were playing pranks while their parents weren't home.

If Tía Amelia had been with Mom, she wouldn't have heard the noise and the doorbell or the pounding on the garage door. If it had been a break-in, she and Mom would have been in trouble. So, no, Amelia is off my list for night stays. I took over one of her nights and Laura took the other.

Laura continues to help Tía Amelia with her needs and with what she can to help with Mom. I truly appreciate what she does to help. If for some reason, she can't take Tía Amelia to a doctor's appointment, she finds someone to help. I've helped her once, but I know I would do it again in a heartbeat.

Is It Only Mamá?

"Mamá thinks she overdosed.
The paramedics delight in her mistake.
What a Holy woman she must be.
Statues all around her. The rosary
close by. They smile!"
– Sylvia R. Merino

As Mom ages, I find she is doing so many odd things. Some embarrassing, some concerning, and some just funny.

Mom loves attention. When we are in a group setting, she will interrupt to give her point of view or simply to change the subject. I do feel badly though, when we start speaking in English and Mom is trying to keep up with the conversation. Finally, she'll announce, "Me no *speakie* English." I don't recall her doing this when she was younger but then again, I probably wasn't around when the adults were into their heavy conversations. After being gone for 21-plus years from my native home, I have forgotten my Spanish and so it is frustrating trying to think of the correct word when speaking to Mom. Then it becomes annoying when

I finally have the words and start talking and Mom stops me in mid-sentence to correct a word I mispronounced and then I lose my train of thought. Sometimes my Spanish comes out meaner than if I had said it in English, so I try to speak Spanish slowly and with a lot of thought before I open my mouth!

Mom also loves to dress up. One time when I was on Mom duty, I left her alone for a couple of hours. This is when she was walking without a cane. She must have played dress-up while I was gone. When I returned, I found her in a knit fitted dress. It was black with white trimming. It was a very pretty dress, but it was so tight on her that her stomach bulged out. I was very much surprised. She is looking at me as if waiting for me to laugh. When I go to sit on the couch across from her, I see a girdle, probably one she wore when she was younger. "Mom, what are you doing? Where are you going?" I finally asked. Then we both cracked up laughing. It was a hot summer day and so I told her that looking at the knit dress was making me warmer, making us laugh more.

After this incident, I began buying her pretty dresses or giving her some of mine that I didn't wear anymore but looked like she could wear with a jacket or a shrug, a short cardigan. She'll wear them to church. Then for fancier events like weddings or parties, since I know her style, I'm the one who goes out looking for something that is in her taste. There are a couple of dresses that are in the fancier category that she has worn to her doctors' appointments. To top it off, she'll put on some foundation and blush and use the blush as lipstick. Mom has no wrinkles and has a nice complexion. She already has rosy cheeks so doesn't really need anything on her face. Sometimes she goes overboard on the blush, so I wipe some of it off.

Then I blow-dry her hair ending with a nicely styled hairdo. She gets many compliments. Just the other day, coming out of her doctor's office, a couple of women who were on their way in stopped to give Mom very nice compliments on her dress. Mom is so proud of herself. She pretends she doesn't care but then she'll remind me of how people like certain dresses she wears.

One time when Tía Fina was staying with her, she tried to help Mom get dressed. Mom insisted on wearing a "dress" that makes her look thinner. When I arrive to pick her up, I recognized the "dress!" "Why are you wearing a night gown?" I ask. It was a nice night gown but not meant to be worn outside of the house.

"So, what, no one is going to know it's not a dress," she tells me, obviously bugged that I would make her change to a dress. But then I remembered that she was going for labs, and they only take 20 minutes max including wait time, I figured this time it wouldn't matter. All was good but, in the future, I asked Tía Fina to put her nightgowns in a drawer and not hang them with the dresses, or to separate them from the dresses if she wanted them hanging. Everyone gifts her nightgowns for Mother's Day, birthdays, and Christmas, and many are very pretty and look better than some dresses.

Then there's the shoe issue. For a long time, Mom was wearing socks with sandals and always has with her casual shoes. Sometimes Mom wears slacks to her doctor appointments. She will wear whatever pair of socks she pulls out of her drawer. Sometimes they don't match her pants, and she will tell me I am too picky, especially when I won't let her out the door until she puts on matching socks. Just recently, she wore a very pretty dress, and I was surprised she was wearing it. It was the dress she wore for her 90th birthday party. That was fine but then I look down and she's wearing Sketcher tennis shoes. I asked Tía Fina why she had those on, and she tells me that Mom insisted on wearing them. I left it at that. She still got many compliments from patients and staff. They were probably thinking, *How cute, she's so modern wearing sneakers with her pretty dress."* And it's true. I see Hollywood stars wearing nice formal dresses with sneakers. So, Mom is more fashionable than I am.

While waiting at clinics to get called into the exam room, Mom gets impatient. I normally find a chair for her, and I leave her there while I go check her in. When I return, she has already studied other patients who just arrived or are sitting close by. She'll whisper (out loud) to tell me about her observations. "Look at that lady over there, it looks like she's crossing the river." I explain that she's wearing ankle pants and that they are in fashion. Then she'll say, "Don't look right now, but that lady has a big butt but what a tiny waist she has." I try to tell her to stop talking so loudly and quit criticizing people. Then she'll tell me that they probably don't understand Spanish. I tell her that she doesn't know that, and I try again to get her to stop talking about the people around her and finally distract her by showing her pictures of her great-grandchildren from my cell phone. Then she's bored and says, "Can we leave now?" I respond with a harsh, "No, you can't leave now, the doctor hasn't seen you." Then she sits back pouting. I'm relieved now that she's finally quiet.

Then the embarrassing part is that she'll say, "What if I toot when I stand up?" I want to die. Poor lady, it's not her fault she has that problem, but in a way it is. She is lactose intolerant and still drinks milk. She also eats yellow cheese. I'm the same but I don't drink milk, and I only eat white, goat, or sheep cheese. I've bought her good cheese, but she didn't like it, so she continues with her yellow or white Jack cheese. At least she insists on shredding her own, except now in her 90's she just cuts a chunk off to put in her burrito. One time she tooted all the way to the exam room. Thank God no one was behind us, and the nurse was way ahead of us. When sitting in the exam room, and after the nurse took her vitals, I pleaded for her to behave, meaning to stop tooting. "I can't help it," she tells me. Then she suddenly struggles to stand up.

"What are you doing?" I ask.

"I'm standing to make sure I don't need to toot," she says and then sits down without tooting and I'm relieved.

This reminds me of a story from one of the people I supported where I worked. She was in sales and always had stories to tell us about her 95-year-old mother-in-law who lived with her and her husband. She recounted that even at dinner she would toot, and it was most embarrassing when they had guests sitting at the table. Then she would go on to tell us that this lady would try to help around the house, but that she would forget to not put her delicate lingerie in the washer. They were to be handwashed, but she would come home to find them in the dryer, either shrunk to tiny things, or some so stretched out they no longer fit. I remember thinking at that time, *"What will Mom be like when she's in her nineties?"* Now I know.

Back to Mom's other incident, one day when she was doing well but shortly after she had started coming out of depression, Chalita called to tell us that Mom was very sick. That her stomach was so upset because she thinks she took too many anxiety pills. It was a new bottle but now the bottle only had a few pills left, yet in the morning it was full. I asked Mom if she wanted me to call 911 because by now, she would not move from her bed. It was about two in the afternoon. I called 911 from my house but was told that Mom had to call from her house. So, they called, and I took off and got there seconds after the paramedics arrived. I walked into Mom's room and found five very handsome paramedics standing around her bed. It was quite comical. Over Mom's bed is a huge, framed picture of Our Lady of Guadalupe of Mexico. On the nightstand is a huge and beautiful statue of Our Lady of Fatima of Portugal with the three children she appeared to. Then on another wall there is a crucifix, and, on her dresser and nightstand, there are prayer cards and books, and her rosary is by her side. Not sure what the paramedics thought but they were so cute about it. The one standing closest to her asked if she wanted to go by ambulance to the hospital even though when they took her vitals, she was fine. Mom chose not to go to the hospital. On the way out, one of the paramedics asked me if I wanted to join their crew! I just laughed!

After they left, I wasn't satisfied that Mom really took too many pills. I went into her kitchen and emptied the container of the anxiety pills and counted them. Yes, there were some missing but then I counted what was in the pill box and those accounted for what was missing in the bottle. So, Mom was confused. She didn't take more than she needed to. When I told her, she was mortified for making such a big deal. Again, her stomach pains were probably from eating what she shouldn't be eating.

There's a man from our church that to this day brings her his slacks to hem or a shirt to shorten the sleeves. He was also bringing his suit coats to shorten the sleeves. Tía Fina whispered to me that Mom shouldn't be doing this for him anymore. Apparently, she damaged a piece of his clothing. She cut too much and then she was struggling with the coat. She finally gave up and told him she would only fix his slacks. We think she just liked having him come over to visit. He is an usher at our church. One Sunday, Tía Amelia saw his name listed under the prayer list for the deceased. They think he has a unique name and who else could it be. I take lightly anything Tía Amelia tells us because she can't hear but this was a written announcement. Mom was skeptical, so one day she dialed his phone number, and he answered. She didn't know what to say and finally just asked where he's been since he has not taken her any clothes to fix. He assured her that he would soon.

A new thing Mom has started, when she knows I'm on my way to help her with her shower on days that I'm caring for her, she is more than ready to get down to business. This is what happens. Usually when I go to Mom's house, I almost always take her snacks, fruit, or groceries if she needs something. This means that I enter her home carrying multiple packages. One day, I saw that she had unlocked the door, so I thought that it was nice of her to do that. Well, when I walked in, she startled me when I almost bumped into her. She was walking straight into the bathroom for her shower. As I'm walking to the kitchen to put the packages on the counter, she is hollering, *"Ven ayúdame."* "Come help me." *Oh, my gosh!* It is all I could say to myself. Then of course, I must drop everything and run over to make sure she's not trying to do things for herself and goes off balance and falls. While she's in the shower, I run back into the kitchen to put things away. This has been ongoing, and I know she is not understanding, or remembering that she needs to wait for me to put things down. One day, I still had my purse around my neck because I had to rush into the bathroom because she was already halfway into the shower. This is dangerous and annoying, but it's become regular, and I am getting used to it.

Mom's stomach continues to bother her. I bought her Tums to take later in the day. One day she was sitting in her recliner with a "feel sorry for me face." She says she feels nauseated, so I asked what she ate. I noticed popcorn on the floor and so I asked how much she ate and find out she ate a whole bag. I gave her three Tums and after a while, she was fine. Before I went home, I hid the remaining microwavable bags of popcorn. Later, I went to her house to find all the cabinets opened. I asked her what she was looking for. "*No se, no lo recuerdo.*" She doesn't remember. Then Laura goes the next day, and Mom tells her I hid the popcorn. Laura texts me to ask where I put it. I tell her and so she gives it to Mom. She sternly tells Mom not to eat a whole bag at once. Laura later tells me that the popcorn will be good fiber for Mom. She had a good point there! I hid it because she had already eaten a whole bag and I knew that if I didn't, she would have another bag as soon as I left.

She also gets eye infections at least two times a year that calls for an urgent care trip. Her eyes consistently water and the ophthalmologist can't do anything about it. She was told to use eye drops. Her eyes are very dry and so that causes the tearing. It doesn't make sense to me but that is what the doctor told us. I have the same problem except my tear ducts were cauterized and that seems to help some with the dryness. It seems strange to plug the tear ducts. Like where do the tears come from? The better way to see it is that the tear ducts suck up the tears the eye produces. By plugging them, the tears are forced to remain in the eye to keep them moist.

Mom is very frugal and always has been. One time when we were in Tucson visiting our families, my husband and I were on our way back home to San Diego, Mom kindly made us sandwiches so that we wouldn't waste time stopping at a restaurant. When we went to eat them, my husband says, "Oh, it's a bologna and bread sandwich!" I didn't get it because we were used to a slice of bologna between two breads lathered with mayonnaise. Ralph then describes his sandwich, that included cheese, tomatoes, and lettuce. Mom must have saved the lettuce and tomato for our dinner. And what does this have to do with Mom?

So, because Mom's eyes water, she is constantly wiping them. She uses the same Kleenex repeatedly. I explain that by using the same Kleenex, she is passing the infection from one eye to the other. I know her well enough to know that she can't stand that she'll need to buy more Kleenex. The next time I went to Sam's Club, I bought her a huge supply of Kleenex. She is better now about using a clean one more frequently than not. I teased her that I hoped she wasn't counting two squares of toilet paper as to not run out sooner than she wanted. She laughs and says, "Oh, Sylvia, I'm not that bad."

Mom's room when paramedics visited her. The bed was centered and her brown rosary is missing here.

Mamá's Hair

"Mamá's hair, it's greasy, flat, not her hair.
Too much purple, not the color. Mamá's too short.
Not tiny, just short, short, short. They can't wash her hair.
Takes, 2, 3, 4 to wash it. Mamá doesn't care,
She sits, they wash, cut, cut, dry, dry. New hair,
new style, Mamá is beautiful."
– Sylvia R. Merino

Before I began styling Mom's hair, I was taking her to get her hair done professionally. One time while there, she had me ask if they would wax her mustache. She cracked me up, but she was serious. Another time, I had bought Mom purple shampoo that is for gray hair. I explained that she needed to keep it in her wet hair for two minutes, then rinse, or whatever the bottle said. Dummy me, I trusted she would remember. Well, that day when I was with her, I noticed her hair looked weighted down and dull looking. "What happened to your hair?" I asked.

"Well, I washed my hair with the purple shampoo like you told me to." And I responded with, "And how long did you keep it in?"

"It's still in!" She replies.

"No! You were to keep it in two minutes then rinse it." I advised she use lots of shampoo the next day when she washes her hair.

Three days after the purple shampoo incident, I needed to take her for a good haircut for one of our niece's weddings. Mom is money tight, so she always washes her hair right before I pick her up for her hair appointment. When the hairdresser began cutting her hair, she calls me over to interpret. "Is it okay if I wash her hair? It's greasy!" I explained what happened and she chuckles and tells me she was glad I told her because she had some product that would strip the grease out of her hair. Mom was fine with it but what happened next was hilarious. Mom is barely five feet tall. She is also hunched-back. When they sit her on the standard chair, her head doesn't reach the basin. Her hunched back makes it more difficult. There were three hairdressers and none of them knew what to do. One suggested using a child booster but Mom wouldn't fit in it. So, then someone thought of a garbage can but that would be too flimsy. Finally, I saw a step stool over by the cabinets where they keep their towels and suggested it. They tried it but two of us had to hold onto it. One hairdresser washed her hair, one held onto the stool on one side, and I held it on the other side. I can't believe they've never had another person like Mom walk into their shop needing their hair washed! I was so relieved when they were done, when suddenly, Mom asks, "Can you wax my mustache?" pointing to her top lip. At least for this one, they sat her up on the chair without the stool.

Laura took her to get her hair cut a few months later. While she was waiting for Mom, she took a picture of her getting her hair cut and sent it to me. We always do this. When I take Mom to doctors, I sometimes send Laura a picture of Mom on the exam table or while she gets her toenails clipped. When Laura took my aunts and Chalita to get their COVID shot, she took pictures of them in line and at the same time the TV station was reporting the lines of people waiting for their vaccination. There are a few pictures we took of Mom when she was grocery shopping, hanging onto the cart. These were videos and you can see her walking ever so slowly. She is unaware that we are doing this, but later we show her the pictures and she scolds us. "Malditas!" she'll scream at us. "You are all so mean!" Yet, afterward, she'll go through the pictures and laugh.

Since it is now too hard for Mom to get around, I take my good shears to her house when her hair gets too long. The first time, I left long hairs at the neckline and so each time I took her to a doctor's appointment, I would clip whatever long hairs stuck out with Dad's old shears.

One day, it took me about 45 minutes to cut her hair. I knew she was getting tired and so I tried to go faster but I wanted to do a good job this time. I thought it turned out just fine! It was shorter than what she wanted, but I felt better when visitors commented on how good she looked with the new cut. The last time I cut her hair, I followed the previous cut but didn't cut as much to keep it at the length she prefers. I stand back and tell myself, *"Not bad for a rookie!"*

This is one of the better pictures of Mom's hairstyle.
The more I practice, the better the results!
This is from her friend's 80th birthday party.

Mom's picture sketched by Mark, my nephew.
It is from one of her bad hair days!!

Reflections

"Mamá stares, far, far away.
No glass ball, just air, air.
Yesterday floating, floating before her.
Today is not here, it is yesterday she sees,
feels, smells, touches. I'm here,
Mamá, don't leave me, not yet."
– Sylvia R. Merino

There are some pictures I've taken of Mom sitting in her recliner, watching her shows. She is focused on the TV, but sometimes I think her mind is somewhere else. I normally sit on the couch to her left and away from her view. I stare at her face sometimes and think of all the experiences and emotions she has gone through: illnesses, sadness, love, and joy. As of this writing, she has lived for 93 years. It must be exhausting, but not really. She did fun things in her life, like her pilgrimages, something so unexpected for a woman who was terrified of heights. For her to trust an airplane to fly her across the globe was a miracle on its own. She used her talent in sewing clothes for her family, friends, and strangers. She enjoyed counseling the engaged couples and she was a catechism teacher at the church.

After I'm done reflecting, I see her uncombed hair and I ask if she combed her hair this morning. Then I ask if she walked for more than the four minutes it takes her to go to the restroom. Then I remind her that she never let us watch TV because we were wasting time. We couldn't listen to the radio either, especially not when we were driving. To this day, I lower the volume when she's in the car. She thinks it's distracting.

Caregiving is a hard and important career. I never in my life thought I would be doing this. The only thing I get out of it is to learn what not to do when I get old and need assistance. Mom never had to care for an elderly person. She always feared she would need to care for Dad if he lived to be in his nineties, sick and bedridden. She has thanked God a dozen times that it never got to that point. With those thoughts and the fears, you would think that she would be easier with those who care for her.

During the years of caring for Mom, I have come across others who share their stories, or the stories of their acquaintances, or some I have personally observed. Some stories are so sad to hear, some are beautiful to witness. Like the daughter who has her Mom's head on her lap and is stroking her hair, comforting her in a most loving and tender way. If I were to attempt to do this with Mom, she would probably push me away and I would be left hurt and with resentment.

In contrast, there's the story of a friend whose young daughter, just beginning her career, works at an assisted-living home. She is not a nurse but an activity coordinator. Her story is that she sees abuse regularly but fears that if she reports it, she'll be fired. This is exactly the reason I will never trust a facility such as this one with any of my elderly loved ones.

Then there's the daughter who left her husband, temporarily, to care for both elderly parents who then became ill, needing more care; she subsequently lost her husband for good. Shortly after both parents had passed, she was diagnosed with an illness that put her in an assisted-living home. This young lady had no life, but in her eyes and in God's eyes she did her duty on earth, and perhaps that was meant to be her life. She never complained and gave all she had, to the parents whom she loved so much.

Mom is stubborn, but I've been told that she's not stubborn, she is just trying to be self-sufficient. She doesn't want us telling her what to do, but in many cases, it is crucial that we guide her; especially when it comes to her medications. Sometimes she flat-out tells Tía Fina she won't take her medication. When Mom does the same with me, I stand by her and tell her that I won't leave until she takes her pills. She rolls her eyes at me and will take them one by one as slowly as possible to get back at me. When she complains that they upset her stomach, I tell her that if she took them with breakfast when she's supposed to take them, her stomach wouldn't hurt. Mom just hates taking her pills and I know my mother-in-law did too, so maybe it's common with the elderly.

While staring at Mom, I get nostalgic. I think of our past lives as a family. The hurtful days when Dad was mean to her, and the days that led to Dad's conversion to become a better person and the joy it brought to Mom. I think of all the losses in her immediate family, like the deaths of her brother at an early age and then her sisters. She clings to those she has left; I know she does even though she doesn't express it.

**These are the three remaining siblings from
Mom's family of seven children.
From left to right, Tía Amelia, Mom, Tía Josefina (aka Fina).**

Mom never talks about her feelings, so I wonder what is going on in her mind. Her eyes are so focused, staring into space. She gives me no sign that she knows I am staring at her. I break her thoughts with a random question about her childhood and she'll tell me what she remembers. Then, suddenly, she'll ask me who brought the fruit on the counter, or whatever I just brought her. "It was me," I tell her, and she'll stare harder and then it's like she's gone deep into a space filled with memories where she might be able to remember. "Why couldn't I remember that?" is what I see written on her sad face. When she realizes she can't remember, her eyes become sad and that's when I begin to get emotional; I quickly change the subject to something she'll remember.

As the days come and go, and I see her regressing more and more, I find myself in a calmer state and more patient with her. I also find myself getting more emotional around her, but I try to mask it to not be scolded for showing it. For now, I will continue to do my job as patiently and as lovingly as I can. So that's what I say now, but you never know what new surprises Mom will hit me with!

Gatherings

"Routines, church, food, gatherings.
Mamá surrounded with family, daughters, sons,
nieces, nephews, sisters, cousins, friends, friends,
and more friends, and the Virgen de Guadalupe stares
down, down, as Mamá prays, prays, prays."
– Sylvia R. Merino

Before we all grew up and began leaving home, we had routines, especially on Sundays. We went to church and sometimes stayed to eat breakfast burritos or bought doughnuts to take home. Then in the evenings it was the fried-chicken dinner that seemed like the whole neighborhood was having. When we got older and started having our own families, and for those who still lived in town, the Sunday dinners continued. This went on for many years even after we moved our parents away from the house, they had lived in for more than 40 years.

After our Dad passed away, in 2004, those Sunday gatherings became less regular, but what remained regular was Easter, Mother's Day, Mom's birthday, and the eve of The Virgen de

Guadalupe rosary. We held these religiously every year at Mom's house. They are now ending, since everyone is getting married and leaving Tucson or other events take priority such as the great-grandchildren's birthday parties, graduations, weddings, etc... Mom will attend some if she feels well, otherwise she stays home, and we report back and bring her pictures.

It is the eve of The Virgen de Guadalupe that I will continue to help with. We tease my sister-in-law, Giselda, that she eventually will continue with this tradition. The Mexican community celebrates the feast day of the Virgin Mary who appeared to Juan Diego in Mexico in 1531, first on December 9th and then on the 12th. The catholic church celebrates the appearance of December 12th. Mom invites the whole family, and sometimes friends, to come pray the rosary. The event is on the Saturday or Sunday closest to the 12th. The tradition is to pray the rosary, then have menudo and hot chocolate with *pan dulce* sweet Mexican bread. We pray the five mysteries of the rosary. We take turns per mystery. The mystery consists of one Our Father, followed by 10 Hail Mary's and ends with the Glory Be. There are five mysteries. We love when the kids take a turn. Their voices are so sweet. Mom relishes having the whole family in attendance but mostly when we all sit to pray the rosary facing the statue of the Virgen that is surrounded by roses and a couple of lit candles. Mom used to kneel but now she sits in her recliner, or a chair when we are outside.

This is when Mom could kneel to pray rosary.

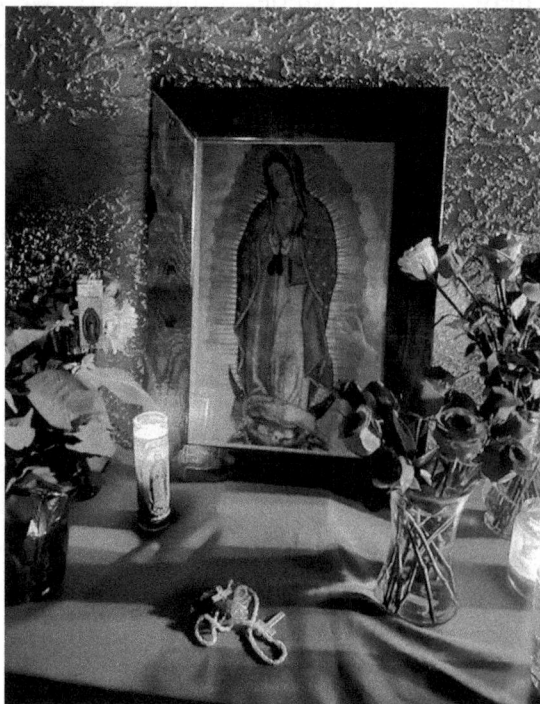

We took alter outside to accommodate more guests.

For her birthday this past year, we invited the family to join us to celebrate Mom at Father Bardo's mass followed with a lunch. Not many family members attended but it was still nice for Mom. Father Bardo is assigned to our old parish. He has always been good to Mom, and she is one of his many mothers. At every parish to which he's assigned, he picks up new Moms. Our mother is one he's kept regardless of which parish he's assigned to. Father Bardo is a nice man, and people are drawn to him. He also owns two dogs and there's always something going on with one or the other. He'll even ask us to pray for one of them who recently had surgery. They are his family. Mom is not a pet person, so she likes to tease Father Bardo about loving his dogs more than his parishioners.

After mass, there were a few of her friends or daughters of friends who have already passed away. Mom couldn't remember some of them until they repeated who they were and who their parents were. There was one woman that took Mom awhile to recognize. The woman had her arms around Mom as she talked to her. She was telling Mom that it was because of her that she went back to church. She had left it for many years, but Mom's counseling had an impact in turning her life around. Mom looked sad as people talked to her. *"What was she thinking, possibly seeing the past? Where did her heart go? Was it sobbing with each memory?"* I'm thinking as she visits with each friend from the past.

At lunch, Mom was very quiet. Father Bardo sat next to her. When we were placing our orders, Father Bardo ordered a margarita and asked Mom if she wanted one. He also asked what she was going to order and was helping her with the menu. She finally asked for a cheese enchilada and water. When the order arrived, she stared at her plate and didn't touch it. She took it home. Everyone else enjoyed their meal and time together. I found out the next day that Mom had been up all-night vomiting. I should have known something was wrong. Usually, I know when Mom is not feeling well. She has this look of pain, like she's holding her breath. This time, I thought she was just feeling melancholy over the friends she saw at church. I'm not sure what we'll do for Mom this year and the next year.

A current picture of Fr. Bardo with Mom and tía Fina.

At Mom's 92-year birthday mass with Fr. Bardo.

Memory and Sneaky

"Mamá forgets, can't remember,
remembers today, not now, now, sometimes
forgets yesterday. Mamá fibs, thinks I don't
know, she's sneaky, but she's wrong.
She was caught."
– Sylvia R. Merino

Mom's memory is slowly slipping away. I wish I weren't in denial. I continue to care for Mom as if her mind were like that of when she remembered everything. Now I can't tell if she is fibbing about something she can't remember, or if she truly can't remember. It has taken a few occasions that were dangerous or just odd to finally open my eyes and heart. With friends and family coming in and out of her home, some have taken note of changes, others think she is just fine, just the same. I spend longer hours or nights with her, so I am seeing the decline much more than the others. I also notice that when something major occurs, the rest of our family become more aware, and they agree with me. Here are examples of what I experienced and still experiencing.

We are thankful that Father Bardo came into our lives. He cares so much for Mom. He visits her regularly. Sometimes he's wearing black pants and shirt with the white collar but a few times, he comes dashing in with his black cassock. It looks like a long dress. He wears it when he visits the sick at the hospital and decides to visit Mom on his way home. He usually visits around breakfast time. Now that Mom isn't as mobile, he'll fix his own breakfast.

One morning when I had stayed the night before at Mom's, Father Bardo called to say he was coming over after a hospital visit. So, I told Mom I would bring father bacon and potatoes from my home and that I would make his breakfast. Well, I still had to go shower, but I assumed that Father was just starting his morning. Forty-five minutes later when I get to Mom's he's in the kitchen frying Mom's egg and he had already eaten. I was somewhat perturbed because I had all good intentions of having his breakfast ready before he arrived. He saw my face and said, "I'm sorry, but your Mom didn't tell me you were coming, or I would have waited for you!" I had to change my composure and told him I would cut up some oranges I had brought with me. He got excited, but I think it was mostly to make me feel good and useful. He later explained that he called from the hospital. That means that he was only 15 minutes away from Mom's house. Mom didn't tell me that. That's how quickly she forgets things.

Mom has good and bad days. On bad days, not knowing it's a bad day, I'll call to ask if she needs something from the grocery store, or I'll tell her I'm coming over later. She'll tell me she doesn't need anything and that I don't need to come and goes on about how much work I must have to do at my own home. She finds excuses to keep visitors away, especially me. I chuckle when I say this because I am the hardest on her, and on these bad days, she wants me as far away as possible so that I don't make her take her pills or force her to eat "food" instead of sweets. If I show up anyway, she gives me little attention, stares straight at the TV and so I get the hint. "Do you want me to leave?" I ask. She always laughs and says "no," but I know she does, so I leave.

Mom does things like this more often, like I'll leave her pills in her pill dish in the morning. There were a few occasions when I would return after two in the afternoon, and she still had not taken her pills, and of course, that annoys me and more so, worries me. If it is past one in the afternoon, I don't let her take them because some of the same pills are repeated just two hours later. I get into terrible guilt trips. Like am I going to kill her by not letting her take her pills late or am I going to kill her by letting her take them back-to-back and overdosing her. I needed a new plan.

Then she thought she was going to trick me by putting a Kleenex over the pill box thinking I wouldn't look. It has taken years to finally get her on a semi-regular schedule; then she started her new thing of refusing to take any of her pills. It was when the doctor looked at her straight in the face and told her, "If you don't take your pills, especially the thyroid one, your head is going to swell, and you will die." Mom's lower lip began to tremble. I thought she was going to burst out crying and felt so sorry for her, but she needed to be told by someone other than family.

Here is another game she just recently began. When she is given a plate of food, she will inspect it and if she doesn't like it, she'll play around with it with her fork. While I watch her eat, she will slowly put the food in her mouth. The minute I turn away to go into another room, she throws the food in the garbage can. The first time she did this, I asked if she ate her food that quickly and she said, "Yes." I go sit on the couch closer to her, and to my surprise, I find the food on the floor. She must have rushed to throw it away before I went back to check on her and missed the garbage can. I didn't know how to react. First it was anger, then I wanted to laugh. All I could say to her is that she can't live off sweets and that she doesn't need to listen to me, then I add, "The doctor will know what you are eating with the lab work." This "doctor" scare works most of the time, but not for long.

There are a few things Mom says or does that test us, but overall, she is our Mom, and she did the best she could to bring us up. She never worked outside of the house, and she never drove. She was dependent on our dad to drive her where she needed to be. Later, when we were old enough to drive, she had us to run errands and drive her to where she needed to be. She also had friends who offered to drive her around, all before Uber existed. For the record, she will never take Uber.

You would think that Mom lived a very sheltered life, but she really didn't. As mentioned before, she traveled out of the country. She can tell us stories of each of her trips. She can tell us about local outings with her friends. What she can't remember are current activities. Some days are worse than others. Not being trained on memory loss, I get confused and sometimes, surprisingly emotional. When she can't remember whether she took her morning pills, I worry, but then when she tells me in the same breath about a show, she was watching just minutes before I walked in the door, I think, *"How can she remember that incident, but she can't remember if she took her pills?"* This frightens me and I quickly begin to run different scenarios in my head as to how I will help her remember to take her pills. My Tía Fina is there all day, and she, too, forgets to ensure she takes her pills. I finally thought that the best way to handle this is to call her to remind her or have Laura go over because she lives closer; but that didn't work. Eventually, Tía Fina caught on that she was the only one who can ensure that Mom will take her pills.

Being your mother's caregiver is hard because you want to do the right things physically, but we forget there is the mental and emotional side too. I've noticed that when Mom can't remember something that she had just mentioned and I ask a question related to the conversation, she'll stare into space as if reaching down deep into her memory bank. She'll stare at the TV, and I only become aware that she is not actually watching the TV when I see it is on a sports channel. There is a soccer game, and totally not something Mom would ever watch. When I asked her if she likes watching soccer, she looked up at me surprised and said she wasn't watching anything. It is times like this that I leave her home physically and emotionally exhausted. If there was some kind of communication, it wouldn't be as bad. Instead, I go home trying to figure out what is keeping her mind so occupied.

Those difficult days are when I feel defeated as she fights me to take her pills or won't put her legs up to prevent her feet from swelling, or when I suggest she wear a better pair of shoes to prevent falls, or when I ask what she wants for lunch and she tells me "nothing" and when she flat-out tells me, "No, I don't want to." Or when she completely ignores me. There is not much more I can do for her on those days. On other days, when her mind is good, I threaten her that the doctor will find in her lab work that she is still refusing to take her medication and eats a lot of sweets and carbohydrates. I worry so much about her health and so I become more forceful, and at the end I feel guilty for not letting her get her way.

I begin feeling more and more like a caregiver than a daughter. When I walk into her house, it's like a switch turns on that says, *"You are now the caregiver, and she is your patient."* She's always sitting in her recliner, so I don't hug her anymore; instead, I'll pat the top of her head or her shoulder. From there, I move like a robot, cleaning her kitchen, picking up Hall's cough drop wrappers, and sweeping crumbs all around her recliner, water plants and asking what she will eat for lunch, and the answer is always, *"No se."* Which means, "I don't know." So now I am the cook and need to think quick as to what to go home to cook for lunch and/or dinner. Then there's the shower routine. Sometimes, I'll add in a manicure and a pedicure. She loves it when I do.

While going through the motions of massaging her legs and cutting her nails, my mind travels to the years that have gone by. Our parents were not affectionate with us but if there was one tiny action you can call affectionate, it became a memory. Mine is the one time, on Christmas Eve, that I was lying on mom and dad's bed while waiting for Santa Claus. Mom came and laid next to me. She rubbed my back and played with my hair. I loved that short moment, and that feeling is one I will never forget. I only hope that Mom will cherish the moments that I spend massaging her legs, feet, and arms.

With my brothers, she is different. She adores them, and they can do no wrong. When I'm around her, she appears to be feeling great. As soon as one of my brothers calls her, she lowers her tone of voice and I can hear her saying that she feels tired, or not well and will continue to speak as if she were dying. When she hangs up, she is back to feeling just fine.

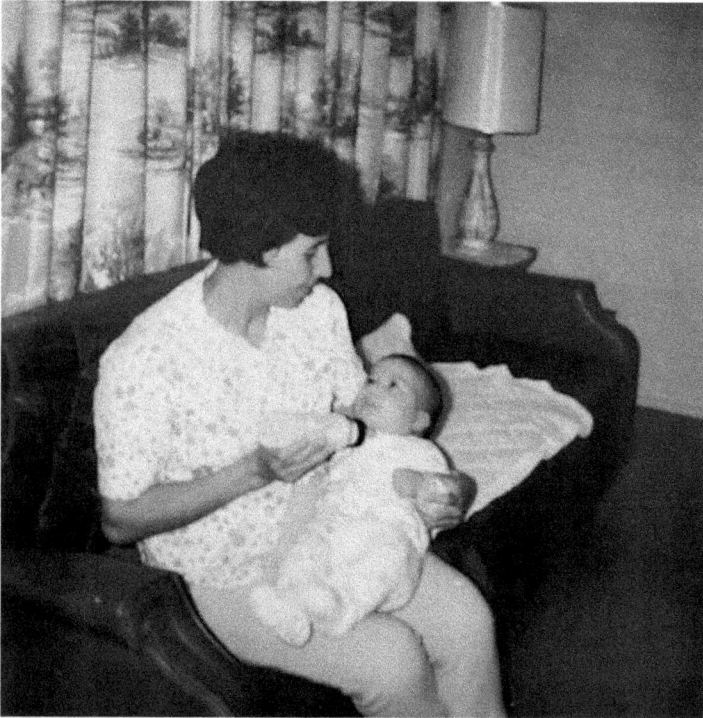

Mom with second son, Jerry.

She also uses them against me. For example, she will talk to one of my brothers about needing something done to the house. Sometimes it's minor and when she mentions these things to me, I quickly stop her from taking any action and I can tell she hates it. She hears advertisements on TV and so she thinks she needs new windows or a new roof. I've come to learn that being a caregiver also means being alert to any strange actions or requests.

One day when I was at Mom's, I noticed she had an advertisement of some sort in her hand. At first, I thought it was junk mail she was getting rid of. She's on the phone with my brother, Jerry. When she hangs up, she sneaks the paper between a stack of books she has on her table. I asked what the call was all about. She made something up that didn't make sense. Later in the day when I'm at home she called to tell me that someone is coming over to fix her roof. I went to her house immediately so she could explain how that came about. She tells me, "A very nice lady and young man came over, and they speak Spanish. They said that hailstorm damaged all the neighbors' roof and that mine looked bad too when they looked at it from the neighbor's house." I asked her for the lady's phone number and told her that I would call her from my home.

I called the roofing company, and the woman was very nice and proceeded to comment about the nice, sweet lady (Mom). I mention that we need the insurance involved and approval for a new roof plus the fact that we had part of the roof fixed just a year ago because the wind had blown away some of the shingles. She told me they needed to replace all the shingles because the new shingles would leave a seam where the most recent shingles were added. When I mentioned insurance, she told me to mention it was hail and wind damage. At that point I realized she was scamming Mom and now me. What she didn't know is that I was going to outsmart her.

Mom's insurance sent an inspector to look at the roof. He requested a representative of the roofing company be present. I was at Mom's house to ensure Mom understood what they told her. The roofing company sent a young man who stood outside the front lawn looking up as the inspector checked things out. At the end, the insurance company told the roofer that Mom's roof was in good condition and wouldn't need any work for a long time. The roofing company representative glared at me but thanked us and left. I then had to educate Mom (again) that she should not talk to strangers about anything or at least she should tell them that she needs to check with her husband. Even though dad is no longer living, she has at times told people at the door that her husband was sleeping. She felt it would deter the salesperson.

From watching commercials on TV and then speaking with friends, Mom decided she was going to switch to Medicare. We explained that her insurance is much better than Medicare. Then she counters that her friends don't pay anything for Medicare. I explain that they do and that when they go to the doctor, Medicare doesn't pay for everything. Mom's insurance is a federal insurance, a rollover from when Dad was living. One doctor confessed that Mom has a very good insurance and went on to tell us that he shouldn't be discussing this with us, but that it would be best she stayed with it. Every year when it's time to renew our insurance, she once again begins talking about switching to Medicare. Thank goodness, her signature is needed to switch to a new insurance company, otherwise, she would have had a friend do it for her!

Mom also forgets that she doesn't go into the carpeted bedrooms because from her many injuries from her falls, she feels unstable. She thinks that her cane will get stuck on the carpet when she least expects it and will fall. One day, I went into one of the rooms and noticed the drawers of the dresser were wide open and the closet doors were left open. No one was at her home that day and so I asked what she was doing in the room. She denied she walked back there and blamed it on Tía Amelia. Tía Amelia had not been there in days. I asked her with a different question. "What did you find in the room?" and she responded that she was looking for a blouse but couldn't tell me which one. I put everything back in order and asked her to please not walk into the room again, but it never crossed my mind that she didn't remember that she was afraid to walk on the carpet. Yes, that is a concern.

Just recently, one early morning, I received a frantic call from my tía Fina. "Your mom is having a breakdown. She's very nervous." "Oh, no, what is going on?" I ask. Tía Fina proceeds to tell me that Mom gave her Visa card number to a man who knocked at the door the previous day and said he would arrive at 8 a.m. to do something and he's still not here. I couldn't hear anymore, I told my tía that I would call back. I had to call my sister, Laura, quickly to have her call the bank to block her card. Laura immediately checked her statement online, and we were both relieved there were no charges. I quickly left for Mom's house and arrived at about 9:15 a.m. I asked slowly and calmly, "Who was the man and what is he doing for you?" She tells me it was a man who will fix her roof and since it is only $38 dollars, she thought it would be okay. Then tía Fina shouts from the kitchen that she told her he was going to exterminate her house. I am so confused. They were mainly concerned because the man said he would arrive at 8 a.m. and he still had not shown up. At exactly 9:30 the doorbell rings. I went to the door and the guy standing there says, "Can I speak to the lady of the house?" I told him, "No. Who are you and what is it that you are doing?" He explained that the company is an environmental exterminator and that they sweep the debris from the roof and around the windows to remove spider webs before they spray. I explained to him that we thought it was a scam, especially since no invoice or receipt, nor a business card was left with Mom. He explained that it was his boss who came to make the deal. I told him the Visa card was blocked because we thought it was a scam. He tells me he will call his boss. I go inside and then it occurred to me that I should give them my phone number so that they would not be tempted to call my mom. When I went outside, the young man was already on the phone with his boss. I walked over and leaned right over him and loudly spoke to the boss that we do not need the service, and that Mom already has regular spraying from the same company she's had for many years. The boss took my phone number. I walked back into the house and within 10 minutes the doorbell rings again. This time it's the boss. He explains that he follows the workers who do the actual spraying. He wanted to know why we wouldn't want to try them out. I clearly told him that we don't need their service. He left and I grabbed my purse and keys to leave. I noticed he parked two houses down. I pull out and he slowly drove ahead of me. He drove very slowly, and I found that suspicious. I memorized his Texas license plate and wrote it down as soon as I got home. I didn't do anything with it, and perhaps I should have called the cops or wherever you call to report a scam. After this incident, I took Mom's checkbook and wallet home with me. This will keep her safe from scammers.

The next week, I walked into her house and found a mess on the kitchen counter. I have all her blank pads, checkbook, and other important papers in a basket. She had dumped the basket because she was frantically looking for her Visa card. As soon as I walked in, she said, "I can't find that thing." "What thing, mama?" I ask. She says, "A man called and wants me to call him back with the card number." He is with the Pope and he's selling a cross. It's from Padre Pio. I love Padre Pio." She says all this as she sadly goes to sit on her recliner. On the coffee table she has more papers strewn and I spot a telephone number.

"Mamá, tell me again, did you call the man, or did he call you?"

"I called him. I want to buy the cross. Can you call him and give him the card number? I can't find the card." I finally got it. She saw the advertisement on EWTN, the Catholic TV Channel, and that's where she got the phone number.

"And how much is this cross selling for?" I asked as she is thinking hard. She tells me, "It is $300 dollars, but it's pure gold."

"No, mamá, you can't buy it. It is too much, and you already have many crosses." She sighed and didn't say much more. This was heartbreaking but at the same time I knew she really didn't know what she was doing. After all, she's the Mom who complains that she doesn't have money!

I explained to her that I have her wallet and checkbook at home to protect her from awful people who want to trick people into giving them their money. I told her the cross was legit, but she really doesn't need something that expensive. She just stared at me with a blank look.

The Daughter Visits

"Mamá, I'm your daughter, hija, hija.
See me, touch me, touch me. Mamá
tell me stories, stroke my hair, touch my skin,
the one you gave me. Count my fingers, toes, one, two, three.
Mamá, kiss me, hold me. I can't reach you, you can't
reach me. I smell you; I hear you; I touch you.
Hear my heartbeat, it's calling for you."
– Sylvia R. Merino

When I go to Mom's house as a guest, and not the caregiver, it is very hard to sit long enough to just chat with her, without thinking as a caregiver. I get such an urge to quickly get up from the couch when I see something on the floor, or to peek in her kitchen, or in her pill bowl. These visits are supposed to be normal, family visits. After a few minutes of trying my best to be the daughter of just a few years ago, I spoil the visit when I ask if she took her pills. If she tells me she did, I don't question her further, but I'm left with doubt. *Did she really take them?*

During these visits, it is more than likely that Tía Amelia will show up and that helps to get conversations going about the past. Tía Amelia is hard of hearing so it's always "Huh?" and we repeat the discussion. Then if my Tía Fina is also there, it gets crazy. It goes like this: I'll ask a question about when Mom was growing up. Tía Amelia will quickly start talking about the experiences because she can remember. Mom enjoys listening to the stories but then when Tía Fina starts adding, Mom will interrupt her at mid-sentence to give her input and then Tía Amelia keeps talking because she can't hear that Tía Fina is now giving her input and I'm just sitting there trying to figure out where the original answer to my question went. It is funny, though!

After a few minutes of these convoluted conversations, I focus on Mom's face and my thoughts drift away into incidents from my childhood under Mom's care. With the lack of affection we received, there was still love expressed in odd ways. Mom wanted the best education for us. She taught us to be polite and respect-ful, not just to her and Dad but to the world. I shift my eyes to Mom's eyes. I see pain and sadness as she struggles to speak of current events. It is emotional for me to continue to guess what she is feeling or remembering. It is hard to openly ask, *"What are you thinking of, mamá? What worries you?"* I am afraid of the answer. I rarely cry but know that her answer will cause a stream of tears. After another 10 minutes or so, I begin to fidget. I get up and tell Mom and my aunts that I need to go home to get going on my to-do's. This time they all stand, and I give them all a hug and walk away. On my drive home, I sigh but I don't cry. I forget about my personal chores, and instead I pray that Mom will be with us a little bit longer.

It's late in the afternoon, when I get home. If only to distract my sadness, I go into my craft room and look to see what I can immerse myself in. I find a rock and paint the first coat. I put it aside to dry and walk back to the kitchen to start thinking what to make for dinner.

This is another day that I didn't get time for painting or writ-ing. I am disappointed and emotionally upset at the same time.

These same feelings seem to add up and it becomes an imaginary thing rather than a feeling. I imagine stones piling up in the pit of my stomach. It's as if one day, my stomach will explode when I can't take the emotions, tasks, and the schedule of caregiving any longer and the stones will come rolling out in one big gush.

When the phone call comes in that Tía Fina is leaving us again, it's almost unbearable. My back stiffens and my lower back hurts and remains painful throughout the days my aunt is gone. *"Is this what all daughters/sons go through when caring for their parents?"* I think it is only me who reacts this way and so then I put more guilt on myself, wishing I could be normal like all the other caregivers.

Smart Electronics – Not For Some

"Mamás' and Papás like mine,
full of wisdom, but not smart,
for smart TV, cell phones. TV and
phones are smarter. Crazy things happen,
screen goes dark, dark. Phone dials wrong person.
Nothing works. What happened to my TV, to my
phone? she asks. She doesn't know anymore, she
feels dumb, but she's not.
– Sylvia R. Merino

When a new version of a cell phone or TV is available, I cringe. Any "smart" TV or cell phone should not exist for the elderly, especially those with dementia, or for not so technically smart people. One of my brothers bought Mom a cell phone years ago and she got rid of her landline. At first, she was able to use her phone for calling us. She occasionally had issues with upgrades or a new feature. Now with her short memory, she doesn't remember how to get to her contacts nor the "most recently called" section. She has called Father Bardo at odd hours when trying to call one of her kids. Thankfully, he is kind and just chuckles over it. Then she dials people through the Facetime feature but doesn't know how to connect. And when the phone rings and the answering button and the speaker button show up at the very top of the screen, she can answer the phone except the phone is on her lap so she can't hear the person calling. We have shown her that she needs to press the speaker button to hear the person or put the phone up to her ear. She tells everyone her phone doesn't work. What she and I agreed on is that if I call and she can't hear me, I will hang up and she is to call me back. She can call back via the regular mode by going into her "Recent" called list. When my Tía Fina is there, she's able to help her. The only problem is that if she doesn't feel like talking to me, she won't call me back.

We don't understand how she knows to silence her phone. We have called many times, and she won't answer it. We worry, thinking she may have fallen and can't get to her phone, so Laura ends up driving over to check on her only to find out that the "Airplane" mode was accidently activated, or the phone was muted.

Recently, things got worse, but I think it's because she was very nervous and anxious over Stephen, our youngest sibling, who had minor surgery that would heal in a matter of a few weeks. Knowing how nervous Mom gets about any small thing, I repeatedly told Mom that her son would be just fine. Soon, I began receiving hang-up calls from Mom. I would immediately dial her back, thinking she had fallen and needed me. Each time, when I called her back, she wouldn't answer my call. I would wait for about an hour and call her back. She then answers and tells me, "I tried dialing Esteban (Stephen,) but it dialed you instead. My phone doesn't work. I don't know what's wrong with it." I respond with, "I'll come over to see what's wrong with your phone." I drive over and try to explain that she is putting her fingers on two names at once and so that's how she's dialing me instead of Stephen.

Mom continues to dial Stephen at odd hours of the day. He probably doesn't mind the calls, but I personally would go crazy. She's worried and so she checks on him constantly. She gets hurt when we (Tía Fina and me) tell her to stop calling him so frequently. She ignores us and continues to dial him whether he answers or not. Well, one morning at 6 a.m. she dials him, but it is Father Bardo who answers the phone very groggily. Mom doesn't apologize nor does she inform him that she meant to dial Stephen. Father thinks that Mom misses him and wants to see him so he tells her he will come for breakfast on Saturday. Later that same day, or I should say night, well past nine o'clock, she rings Father Bardo again. This time, she does tell him that she meant to dial Stephen. When I heard about these calls, I texted Father Bardo and apologized for Mom, explaining that she was trying to dial Stephen and not sure why she kept misdialing. He writes back, "That's because we are both her youngest, spoiled sons." Father is too nice.

Many have asked why we don't buy her a medical alert necklace. We could, but she won't remember how to use it. If she fell during a time that we leave her for an hour, she would freeze or panic and would forget what she needs to do with the device. So, Laura and I have more reason to make additional trips to Mom's house when Tía Fina is out of town.

Mom also likes to listen to CDs. She knew how to handle the old tape recorder and play the recordings so she thought a CD player would work the same. She asked Jerry to buy her a small, easy-to-use CD player. He taught her how to insert and eject the CD. He taught her how to play it and how to stop it. One day, as I was getting out of the car, I heard music. It was a Mexican artist she likes listening to. The music was on full blast. When I walked in, she quickly asked me to lower the volume because she didn't know how to. Then she asked me to show her how to do everything Jerry had already shown her. The next time I go over, the CD is on replay, and she tells me it's been like that all morning. Eventually, she decided she would stop playing CDs and only watch TV shows. I thought of showing her how to use Spotify, Pandora, or YouTube to get her music, but that would be another mistake. I could see her running her battery because she wouldn't remember how to turn the music off.

Buying her a smart TV was the worst purchase we ever made. She is completely lost with the two remotes and the icons that appear on the TV screen. She uses a cable company, so she has a cable box remote and the TV remote. One has a keypad for the channels, the other doesn't. One has a volume button that works, the other doesn't. My husband set the TV volume for her, so it never needs changing. When someone calls, Mom knows to use the "mute" button but then forgets she needs to press it again to unmute it. Sometimes instead of the "mute" button she presses one of the other buttons and the TV goes blank. Since then, we get calls at odd hours asking if we can go fix her TV or show up at her house and she's staring at a blank TV. I have done everything I can to teach her how to use the remote controls. I've put round colored stickers on the buttons to use. I've taught her not to touch any of the other buttons. I've also created a two-page manual with pictures in both Spanish and English. This one was more for my siblings and myself, since sometimes I've had to call my husband to get us out of a dead-end. Poor Mom!

We bought her a smart recliner with a remote control. At first, she didn't want to use the recliner feature. The first night she had the recliner, it happened to be my turn to spend the night with her. I reclined the chair and brought her feet up to where she wanted them. They were not level to her heart, but she had already agreed to that level, and I didn't want to discourage her by making her do something different. In the morning, I got up early enough to help her work the remote so she could get off it. Her feet were more swollen than I've ever seen them. It scared me. After her shower, I made her go back to the recliner and this time I reclined her feet as far up as I could, so her feet were level to her heart. After about an hour, her feet were back to normal.

The next night, Jerry was to stay with her. I asked him to be sure he reclined the recliner as far as it would go. All went well. On the third night, Stephen stayed with her, and Mom refused to sleep on the recliner. Mom was probably in one of those bad day moods. She won that night and slept on the couch.

When I saw Mom the next day, I told her the doctor will be angry when she sees her swollen feet and that I will explain to the doctor why. But Mom continued to sleep on the couch. Sure enough, at the next appointment, when the doctor saw her red, swollen feet, she asked if she had a recliner. "Yes, she does!" I enthusiastically replied. I went into the story of her not wanting to use it. The doctor stared into her eyes and said, "You need to use the recliner to raise your feet above your heart. Your feet are too swollen and so you must raise them!" Since then, Mom has reclined but the first few times, she couldn't work the remote. She would call out early in the morning to whomever spent the night with her. She needed help getting the remote off the reclined position. This remote is the only one she has learned to use. *"Praise the Lord!"* I thought to myself, that one morning when she proudly told me that she didn't need help with it. She had mastered it!

Fear of Tomorrow

"Mamá is here. Tomorrow she may not be. Today she is here.
Love her, bring her flowers, roses, carnations,
snap dragons; bright ones, red, yellow, purple, pink,
orange, the colors in a Crayola box. Mamá forgets but she can
see, touch, smell. Love her, love her one more time,
today, tomorrow like yesterday.
She can't remember."
– Sylvia R. Merino

I know there will come a day when Mom departs this materialistic world. That's if we don't go before her. She will leave us
with memories, some good, some not so good. That thought is
always there. I pray that my heart won't break into pieces when
she does go. If I fall apart, it won't be because I fear where she'll
end up. She is a good woman. She has prayed all her life. She is
close to God and all the heavenly saints and angels. Father Bardo
hears her confessions. *"What can this woman confess?"* She rarely
leaves the house. Maybe she confesses the small lies she tells us
about, or some of the X-rated cases coming out of the *Doctora*,

the program she watches. There is nothing more that she can confess unless it's a sin to criticize her daughter or people in the waiting room at the clinic. Other than those small things, I think God will forgive her and take her straight on up into the heavens.

I will break down thinking of what I didn't say or what I didn't do. I will break down for never knowing what she suffered in silence. I will break down for never hearing her stories of how she came to love her husband. I will break down for never experiencing that touchy feeling from that Christmas Eve of long ago. I will break down knowing I lost my main audience who laughed at my silliness. I will break down from emotional exhaustion.

As my dentist worked putting a temporary crown in my mouth, he mentioned that just recently, his elderly Mom had lived in another state and had family checking on her, but they, too, lived far or even in a different city. It was becoming harder to communicate and care for her from afar. She was brought home to a local nursing home. That's when they learned she had dementia. It was an eye-opener, and he said it was more of a learning experience for them, than for his mom. It's true, the patient doesn't realize they have dementia, so it's up to the caregivers to understand their needs. What struck me the most is when he told me that you can no longer argue over small things. Just take each day with kindness, gentleness, and patience. He finished it off with, "You don't want to live the rest of your life thinking of the bad days." I will forever remember this small discussion while I had my mouth wide open, not being able to contradict him, nor respond, other than letting his words sink in.

This is the beginning of the end. I knew it could come today, tomorrow, or 10 years from now. Mom is in her last years. I can see the changes in her demeanor. Mom always loved to dress up. In her earlier years, in pictures, you can see her in dresses and heels, sweeping the back porch. Then later wearing pants and nice shirts and for church nice dresses. She made most of her clothes until we worked and bought her new clothes for her birthdays and Mother's Days. I find myself constantly buying her something or other. I am in denial. I want her to be the younger Mom, but she won't wear them. She lives in her nightgowns unless she knows a non-family member is visiting her or has a doctor's appointment.

She is forgetting more and more. When one of us (her daughters) takes Mom a gift, she forgets who gave it to her. When we leave a bag for one of our sisters, she looks at the bags sitting on the table in the entry way, constantly asking what the bags are doing there and who are they for, even after we had just explained. It used to frustrate me, but now I just repeat what I had explained minutes before.

I know that soon enough, she will not be allowed to stay home alone, not even for a few minutes. I tell Mom that it is a good thing she can't walk very well, otherwise, she would be running around outside, causing more falls. The physical therapist that helped her at the hospital told Mom that we will need to wrap her up in bubble wrap. I had to explain this to Mom. She found it funny only after a few minutes of trying to understand what bubble wrap was.

We have spent 12 years of caring for Mom off and on, and I can hardly believe it. It has only been a couple of years of closer and longer care. Since Ana can't share in the sleepovers or food turns with Mom, we gave her the responsibility of preparing for Mom's funeral — only the church services. Laura and her husband will handle picking out the casket. We were told that Ana and I picked a cheap coffin for Dad. We thought it was nice! Ha! Mom has already picked out the music she wants at her funeral. Ana is also having discussions with her on the readings she wants at the funeral mass. We know which priests will be present at the services. They are Father Bardo, her adopted son, and the other is the priest who Mom and Dad worked with at their old parish. It feels so strange to plan a funeral for a person who is alive and doing relatively well. Yet, not planning may be more hurtful, afraid that we didn't do Mom's funeral services justice.

For many years Mom would tell us she was dying. This went back to when we were toddlers, and it continued to adulthood. We caught on that Mom was afraid to die, even though she denied it. In these last few weeks that I've been with her off and on, I have heard her mention her dreams of her mom and dad speaking with her. Just two nights ago as she was falling asleep, she had the thought that it was time to die and she said, "Take me now." At that, I said "Take me with you."

I know I'll miss her dearly. As it is, I miss her when Tía Fina is home with her and I'm not there doing my normal chores as a caregiver. I still visit and help where and when I can. I try not to think of the day Tía Fina will call to say Mom didn't wake up. For now, Mom is alive — maybe not fully in mind, but she is here with us. Her kids are all here, and we will do what we need to do. Our brother from Minnesota occasionally sends her flowers. She proudly tells us, *"Ricardo me envió flores."* "Richard sent me flowers." We will continue to show her pictures of her grandchildren and great-grandchildren who she delights in seeing, especially those who are far away. We will do what pleases her to an extent!

We never know how one will leave this earth. With that said, I think it is appropriate to add this true story of a friend who was a caregiver for an elderly lady. She gave me permission to tell it in my own words. I wrote it in a prose form:

The Caregiver's Final Services

For months I fed her, administered her medicines,
Bathed her, dressed her, brushed her white hair,
Manicured her nails, massaged her feet.
A quiet routine with few words said between the two.

When her routine broke, for two days Rosa refused
to bathe, be combed, and dressed but today, Rosa
lays out her best dress, asks for the decorative soaps as she
slides into a tub of water and jasmine oil.

By candlelight, I gently bathe her, lulled by the
sound of the trickling water
and the flame of the candle.

Bath over, I dry her, dress her in her undergarments
and proceed with her routine.

I sit on a stool, massage her feet,
surprised when Rosa's soft wrinkled hands
cup my face forcing me to stare into her old, tired eyes.

"You have been good to me.
Thank you for your tender and loving service. I love you so much."

Pouring tears, I continue to dress Rosa,
Ensure she takes her medications.
I call a cab to take her to a casino, her favorite place.

This evening, I found out, Rosa passed away.

I pray that when Mom goes, it is not when I'm performing caregiver duties, but instead, while visiting as the daughter and she as my mother —not the patient.

Mom, at one of her earlier birthday parties.
Keep the birthday candles burning, mamá!!

Also by Sylvia R. Merino

Unraveled: A Journey Led by Faith and Hope

Acknowledgements

Many thanks to my sister, Laura, for reviewing my work and pointing out events that were not quite accurate. I especially thank her for taking it upon herself to do random chores around Mom's home as she sees the need when she's not caring for her grand-children or our tía Amelia.

Thank you to my friend, Kathi for reading the very first draft to correct my Spanglish to pure English!

Additionally, the ongoing assistance and contributions with Mom from my siblings, Ana, Stephen, Jerry, and Richard, are very much appreciated. The unwavering support they demonstrate is undeterred by work schedules, and long distance. I especially thank the boys when they are called to fix a broken toilet, kitchen faucet, or mowing the lawn. Shoutout to Stephen for keeping up with Mom's sweet tooth with pan dulce. I especially get a chuckle when Mom tells me he specifically tells her, "Don't tell Sylvia." and each time, that's the first thing she tells me!

I thank Cecilia, our family friend, who is always willing to help us with "mi Teresita" (as she refers to our mom) by taking a night or two with our mom when needed. She also spoils our

131

mom with her favorite "caldo de queso" (cheese soup), and her annual "flan" (caramel Mexican custard) for her birthday. She is our angel.

Finally, I'd like to express my sincere gratitude to my husband for teaching me patience and for once again, supporting me in my writing. I am sorry for not hearing his conversations when I'm deeply concentrating on my stories, and he must repeat them ever so patiently.